Fidelma Cook's
FRENCH LEAVE

(or yes, I'll have another vin rouge, s'il vous plaît)

Fidelma Cook's
FRENCH LEAVE

(or yes, I'll have another vin rouge, s'il vous plaît)

macdonald media publishing

First published in May 2009 by
macdonald media publishing,

22 Roxburgh Road, Paisley, PA2 0UG, Scotland.

info@macdonald-media.co.uk

ISBN: 978-0-9553126-3-2

ISBN: 0-9553126-3-9

A CIP catalogue record for this book is available from the British Library.

Design and typesetting: Cameron Heggie

Cover: Iain Leckie

Printed and bound by Thomson Litho, East Kilbride, Lanarkshire, Scotland.

For my son Pierce, with love.

Prologue

I'VE always been one of those people who sense things just before they happen. It has saved me on many an occasion. So when the Managing Editor of the Mail on Sunday phoned me, I knew he was about to do what he did just before he did it.

His voice trembled as he spoke and I felt sorry for him - although it was just for a fraction of a second. I was being made redundant... no, correction, as he was at pains to say, my job was being made redundant... not me.

At 56 years old, my time was up. Of course there were procedures to go through – meaningless. Other jobs could be offered within the group - nonsense. Negotiations, conversations, blah, blah.

The plain fact was I was too expensive, too under-used and, for one of me, they could get three kids these days. No contest. Had I but known it, I was a precursor of what was to come - the credit crunch, the global crisis, the end of the known world of our secure well-paid jobs.

As I sat at my hand-made elm tree kitchen table in my

heavily-mortgaged Georgian conversion in Glasgow, I didn't know whether to laugh hysterically or cry. As I'm no good at either, I opened a rather fine bottle of red, lit a fag and pondered my life. It wasn't good.

My overdraft was standing at around £6,000. I had two or three loans and I was paying almost £2000 in mortgage a month and with several re-mortgages, barely owned the front door and hall. There were a few credit cards, which were being paid off at the bare minimum, maxed almost to their limits.

I had a cleaner; a couple who came to take away my laundry and dry-cleaning; a company sports car removed for service when required and the obligatory large expense account. When called out of town to do a story, I paid for someone to pick up Portia, my dog - an Afghan Hound of course - take her to kennels, look after her, and return her to me groomed and perfect.

And I had a black American Express card. Invitation only. For the world's big spenders. In theory I could buy a Ferrari without being challenged as to my credit-worthiness, even though I hadn't enough real cash, in truth, to buy a handbag from Primark.

Don't think I was even touching close to the big name columnists' league in cash terms - thousands and thousands of pounds under. But, I was doing pretty well by 'Fleet Street' standards for, let's face it, very little, when compared to those in the real world.

We, my newspaper friends and I, used to play a dinner party game which involved imagining how we would appear in a centre spread if 'we' turned 'us' over.

I could see it now in my newspaper's classic drop-intro style:

'To those who regularly saw her in the city's finest restaurants, Fidelma Cook appeared to have it all. Witty, wry and possessor of an enviable contacts' book, she was the acknowledged doyenne of Scottish journalism.

'Indeed one young adoring reporter dubbed her the 'Marianne Faithful' of female journalists, an icon who'd been there, done that; the woman who played the boys at their own game and won.

'The lucky handful invited to her exquisite first floor apartment in Glasgow's exclusive Park district were sure of good food - catered; good gossip - in-house; and decidedly good wine - Oddbins. Smoking was compulsory.

'In her deep, throaty voice - once dubbed the sexiest voice in journalism by Alex Salmond, the SNP politician and now Scotland's First Minister - she frequently joked that her life was just 'a house of cards'... but few believed her.

'Today they are realising they should have taken her at her word. For in just 24 hours the façade of Miss Cook's life has crumbled to dust. And visible is a woman of uncertain age with no discernible future.'

Well, we always pushed it to the limit. Am I asking for pity? Don't be ridiculous. Of course not. And do I feel just a little embarrassed by my earnings? Actually, I don't. I wanted to be a journalist since I was ten years old. I worked bloody hard at being one from 18 years old. I was a natural; I loved it and because I was good I more than earned the money editors were prepared to pay to have me on-side.

A woman of my time I started work in mini-skirts, ended in Armani trouser suits and even won a couple of awards along the way. Despite living 18 years with George, the man who fathered my child, I never married. Frankly I could never see the point, never having had any desire to be kept in any way. And no-one ever did keep me, except me. But I insisted our child went to public school even though there were no trust funds to aid the ultimate £22,000 a year it cost us after tax.

When I left his father, I moved into a flat – the Georgian conversion – which was totally mine. I dropped two stone, having become happy again, discovered the menopausal joy of sports cars and wicked black leather jackets and partied all over the city.

Those are the bare facts. Honestly, I'm really a better person than the above makes me out to be. But that is/was the stark reality of my life. I enjoyed the cash I earned, the ludicrous amounts of accessible credit it gave me and when the Managing Editor made that call... it was all over. My house of cards collapsed.

So, here I was. What do I do next? Where do I go? How do I live without a monthly income? Without an expense account? How do I live when even my credit cards start rejecting me? In tabloid terms, an icy hand gripped my pounding heart.

My initial reaction was to call my friends, Peter and William, who arrived with a massive Indian carry-out. Counting calories seemed suddenly a touch futile. As we swallowed more red wine, chewed pakoras and garlic chilli-chicken, I flew high on my future.

At one stage plastic surgery seemed the best idea so that I could re-invent myself as my abandoned daughter and start all over again. We drunkenly discounted it on pain and financial grounds and the fact that with my memory shot anyway, I'd never remember the memories from the age I was meant to be.

Eventually, half-cut and red-eyed, I told them: 'F**k it. I'll go to France.'

Being gay, they fulfilled the stereotype and shrieked: 'No!' loving the dramatic gesture.

'Oh yes, I will,' I told them. 'Can't afford to live anywhere else. And anyway you can still smoke in restaurants there.'

On such reasoned arguments are all major decisions made. We drunk-dialled or texted everyone we could think of to announce the news. The ones I'd only just phoned several hours earlier to tell I was redundant.

By morning the e-mails and texts were rolling in. 'Go, girl... live the dream,' was the thrust of them all. Dream? Dream? What dream? Merde. Girl? I wished.

In the whirlwind that followed I was approached by The Herald and asked to write a weekly column for the Saturday magazine as I 'followed my dream.' I hadn't the heart to tell them it was actually the only option for a woman who had lived life on a financial precipice and was now totally up the creek, without the paddle, and even worse, without the canoe.

What follows is based on those columns, without which I wouldn't have believed all that happened. Or, let's be really honest, remembered.

Chapter 1

I'M plunged into darkness halfway up the shallow-stepped stone staircase. One hand is dragging my bag, the other clutching the rail hauling myself upwards when the light's time switch releases.

Bugger. The door is up there somewhere and another push button light is undoubtedly down the hall from it. In the pitch black, the only sound is the high pitched whine of a middle-aged woman who is still afraid of the dark and the laboured breathing, interspersed with the dry cough, of an unrepentant smoker.

I'm in two-star France where every last centime is counted and none is squandered on guests' comfort and certainly not on lights to guide their way up three flights of concrete stairs.

I'm learning to drop the ludicrously heavy, though beautiful Biggs bag; rough suede, leather corners, separate compartment for shoes; half-way up each set of stairs to give myself a little extra kick-off, sans luggage, to hit that next switch on cue.

But, by the time I've smacked it down; run and fumbled with the bedroom keys , well, the bloody light - way back down the corridor from my door - has clicked off again.

Depending on how far I've driven, how tired I am, how sick to death with all of this I am, I will react in one of two ways. Both involve numerous curses directed at everything from the bloody door to the bloody hotel, or the bloody keys. The universe. My ex-editor. Every person I've ever hated or vaguely disliked.

Anyway, one reaction will see me pathetically slumped against the damn door wishing I could just wail, like we women are apparently prone to do. The other sees me grasping my way back down the hall to find the buggering push-button bloody switch for another assault on the sodding door.

Either way, eventually and inevitably, I open the door to the now depressingly familiar pink emulsioned walls, green carpet, harsh overhead lights, sad little pile of out-of-date tourist brochures and the ubiquitous lace curtains.

And then I sit on the bed and wonder yet again what the hell I am doing here and wish I could howl out loud. THIS IS NOT MY BLOODY LIFE. I unleash another string of curses, shockingly aware how unbelievably undignified and immature my behaviour is. How spoilt, rotten, pathetic and very embarrassing.

After all, I am, to put it nicely, a woman of a certain age. A woman who had a life, a career - who had it all. And now I'm lying on a counterpane in a two-star French provincial hotel staring at a pink ceiling and swearing like a squaddie or an hormonal teenager.

I am 56-and-a-half. A journalist, a mother and someone

whose well-heeled life has just gone down the redundancy pan. I have several credit cards in debt, a few loans, a large overdraft and a Glasgow flat, which may or may not be sold.

In my handbag is the ultimate black American Express card which, technically, gives me enough clout to circumnavigate the world without a credit check. It is by 'invitation only' to the high-fliers who would need a briefing note to understand 'counterpane,' never mind lie on one.

It is the last card standing. I clasp my it to my bosom. At least someone/something still values me. (In the sane bit of my brain I know it will only keep loving me if I pay the £650 a year subscription every October.)

So, here I am once more, on top of a bed in a French provincial hotel of unbelievable ugliness in search of a life I can afford; fleeing from the one I no longer can. This time it's Nerac in the Landes, an hour and a half west of Toulouse.

The furniture in this room is heavy, dark brown and what we could kindly call Victorian. The wardrobe looks ready to topple under its own weight and seemed to sway slightly when I peered inside earlier.

These days I'm so freaked out in my new life that I check everything to make sure no horrors lurk within. I am so far outside my 'comfort zone' I'm convinced monsters lie in wait everywhere apart from five-star hotels. Most times I'm just vainly searching for a hair-dryer.

One harsh centre light illuminates the bedroom's vast proportions and lace curtained windows. Before climbing onto the hard, high bed, I had pulled back a lacy corner to gaze on the empty street leading to the square.

It was only 10pm and, as I'm learning to expect in the South West of France, not a soul stirred, not a dog howled, not a cat prowled. I'm expecting the children of the corn to march down Main Street any second. Or maybe Britt Eckland's body double will start banging on the walls thinking the virgin policeman is having hot sweats on the other side. The only hot sweats here, dear, are post-menopausal. Oh God!

It is now 10.15pm. Outside, plastic Santas climb on ropes up the sides of at least five shops and houses; a few strings of star-shaped lights flash on and off their joyful greeting - colourful accompaniment to the white lights dotted through the trees on the run up to the square.

Christmas trees with slightly tawdry bows of red and gold can just be vaguely glimpsed through the odd shop window. It would all be rather jolly and festive if it weren't February, Christmas wasn't long over and the first stirrings of Spring shoots weren't showing in the window boxes.

Now I'm wondering if I've wandered into Brigadoon and this place has emerged through the mist on its 100-year breakthrough into the world. Maybe I've entered the Village of the Damned? Or is it the Invasion of the Bodysnatchers?

These days the oddest thoughts run through my mind; usually involving black and white films where the last person standing leaves your ears ringing with her shriek. Often I am that person.

Through the bed-head wall I can hear a man snoring, and pass a few minutes counting the pause between the ratcheting death rattles – a bit like counting between the thunder and the lightening.

After every fifth rich, rolling vibrating wave, there is a longer, rather disturbing interlude, which has me sitting up straighter in heightened anticipation. Thankfully the silence ends with a choking, gasping gulp of air before my man settles back to his regular five waves.

I'm feeling quite protective now of the poor soul and, once I've established his pattern, I can relax. Maybe even sleep, lulled by the irregular, regular rhythm.

At least it's company of a kind and much more acceptable than the couple who made love twice (3.10am and 5.30am) loudly, in the room next to mine in Toulouse the night before. I did not count between the 'oui's' and 'Dieu's', but noted with interested detachment how banal and universal are the words of climactic sex.

I did, as a sort of reflex action, find myself counting out loud each thrust which slapped their headboard against our shared wall. There were three of us in this tryst. I prayed he was a premature ejaculator and that it would be all over pretty quickly. He wasn't. Lucky for her, not so for me.

Idly, I'd mused on what sort of a couple would be having so much sex in such a grotty hotel in such a beautiful city. Their voices sounded old, not young, but he obviously had a bit of stamina.

According to the glossies I had to buy in search of story ideas in my old life, the 50s are the new 40s, even the 30s. And those women like me who are liberated, free from husbands/partners, with grown-up children and allegedly loaded with dosh - are totally up for it.

Apparently my generation are out and at it nightly. Poised, liposuctioned, botoxed and unafraid to slip on a biker jacket and a pair of Manolo's we're swinging our waxed, tanned legs and spiky ankles in every chic bar in town.

And true, when I went out in my Prada heels, flicking my tanned ankles, I saw these women quivering out of basque tops (D&G, black, pink bows) licking their thinning lips at coked up footballers; slobbering into champagne flutes.

Personally I just thought they were sad old slappers and thanked God my only two addictions were red wine and fags. Did I burn my bra, worship the blessed Greer and beatify de Beauvoir to be an easy lay under the guise of baby boomers' sexual rights?

Let's be honest here and kill this myth. Unless you're really, really drunk, blind, or scarily self-centred, why would you want to strip off at our age? Mingle all that sagging, crêpey skin with another's greying flesh and share a king-size with no room to star-fish when the flushes peak?

Trust me. Do not believe even the posh tabloids. Most women of a certain age are quietly happy to be celibate, lusting over Johnny Depp and secretly terrified he'd ever turn up and ask them to go on top. Gravity. Think about it. Not a good upward look.

Anyway, let's get back to counterpane musings and my real life before this one in French provincial misery. Once upon a time - just a few months ago actually - I would have been in a very different hotel room. A porter would have led me through plush corridors; well, but softly, lit. After exiting a walnut or glass panelled lift, he would slot a card into my bedroom door, discreetly switching on several side-lamps with a sleight of the hand.

A wave towards the bathroom would reveal granite or marble tops with a carefully piled tower of springy white towels. Shampoos, bath oils, conditioners, would be arranged in perfect symmetry.

I wouldn't need to check the television with its soft music and welcoming 'Good evening Miss Cook,' to know it had every channel I could ever desire and far more than I ever would.

If book-less, the leather-bound hotel guide and local interests brochures would keep me amused. The room service menu would cater to every wish from 'fish 'n' chips' in today's 'Times' to sushi or couscous.

On a coffee table would sit a miniature decanter containing two small sherries, paired with a shortbread biscuit. The latest magazines would be spread before me, all lifestyle and luxury; boys' toys and discreet plugs for teeth whitening and plastic surgery clinics. One's eyes, at a certain age, are drawn, for some strange reason, more strongly to these particular advertorials.

The mini-bar, hidden behind a seamless panel under the vast flat-screen television, would reveal a bountiful array of alcohol and chocolate. I expected, and accepted it, as my due. I had worked hard for it, succeeded in a male-dominated industry and was working for the only newspaper left in the country, which had the will (and the cash) to pay for the best reporters and the best stories.

I deserved it and I wasn't paying. It was all on expenses. All I had to do was deliver. Usually I did.

Tonight, naturally in my bizarre new existence, there isn't

even the consolation of a mini-bar or Sky News. I've finished reading my book and there isn't a glossy mag in sight. The bathroom is a dark, vomit-pink hole with cracked tiles and grey grout. It's a cold, barely functional space.

I forgo the 'luxury' of a bath, using the threadbare towel and my forefinger to rub on the minute square of soap making enough froth to wipe off my eye make-up under the florescent light. In this bathroom, in this mirror – and in this mood – merde, I look every one of my certain number of years.

I finally understand what a turkey neck is as it wobbles back at me as I stare at the woman I've become. Squinting sideways I see at least two chins and, dear God, I've finally got the 'Chucky' mouth… the two lines, which on the ventriloquist's dummy open the mouth.

I try smiling to see if it improves. It does. But I cannot walk around with this manic face just to hide the 'Chucky' lines. I'd be certified. I frown, grimace, gurn, to see just how bad it is. It is seriously, seriously bad. My face has collapsed virtually overnight along with my life.

I decide to stand sideways to see what the whole profile and body outline look like under the harsh glare of the fly-spattered strip. I breathe in. I breathe out. Both are equally horrendous.

In my usual hotels, draped in the white towelling robe, bathed in the pinkish glow of soft 'ladies' lighting, at least I have the illusion of being fit to be seen in public.

Flicking off the light, I crawl back into bed, light another fag and ask the pink ceiling – so this is living the dream is it?

Is this really what the vast majority of Brits fantasise about? What around 500,000 have already done?

Moving to France to create a languid, wine-soaked life, I have to remind myself that I'm 'living the dream.' As the song goes: 'No-one said there'd be days like this.'

Or nights in this case.

Chapter 2

IT all seemed so easy at the start of the summer. A snap decision to finally put my money where my mouth had been for years even though I'd never once engaged brain in the thought.

Often I could be heard telling people that if and when I were made redundant I'd just move to France. You know… for the culture, the food, the wine, the sun. Indeed, I'd say at certain times, I'm tempted just to go now.

'Obviously you love the country?' acquaintances would ask, deeply impressed by my drawl. 'You must spend a lot of time there?' I'd nod earnestly with the sort of smirk which implied every waking moment of my non-working life was spent living la vie Française, but omit to answer that apart from a couple of ski-ing trips, I hadn't been in years.

It was all a glorious pipe-dream, pure mouth-music, now rubbed into technicolour awareness by every television programme showing a life in the sun; every book with a sunflower on the cover.

Sure I was discontented and slightly off-kilter. There was nothing more to do to my rather lovely Glasgow flat; I knew everybody that apparently mattered and I would be sent invitations to most events to socialise with the same 100 people who attended every opening, every year and came out with the same predictable sentences year after year.

Gradually I was running out of steam, energy, desire, hunger and ambition. Was this it? Was this what middle-age – galloping old age – felt like? Living alone apart from a neurotic, hysterical, but very beautiful Afghan Hound and mother of a high-maintenance 23-year-son who has never forgiven me for failing to make him a trustifarian. I had a premonition that life could not go on as it had.

Actually, the old me – the young me still buried in here somewhere - hoped it wouldn't go on. But the me I'd turned into was terrified it might not. Despite a senior position in the Mail on Sunday with a very healthy salary plus lavish expenses, I was permanently in debt, over mortgaged, juggling credit cards and, in truth, far too relaxed about it.

The black cloud of debt wouldn't have concerned me too much – I'd lived that way all my life – if a combination of career malaise and ever-increasing newspaper cutbacks hadn't left me feeling rather vulnerable.

In truth I had it very cushy. I didn't go into the office. I worked from home and justified my existence by sending in numerous ideas (most of which were now rejected). I half-believed the constant assurances from my London boss that it was just a difficult time to get stories into the paper.

The fact that Scotland had few kiss-and-tell superstars (if any) - the mainstay of all papers these days - did not help. Neither did the growing number of my apparently unwanted and therefore unpublished stories.

Actually I knew - in an internet world of plummeting circulations - I was being sidelined as a luxury the paper could no longer afford. I would wake up each morning with that sickly, stomach-churning dread of the day to come. No stories. None that grabbed them at any rate. No call from London to catch a plane to chase a 1500 word spread with picture by-line.

And so it becomes a spiral of defeat. One good story lifts you back up to that plateau of success and the mastery of your craft; none, to the depths. Everything is questioned; even my ability, my 'news sense', which had got me this far in the first place. Having spent my life utterly and joyfully being defined by my job, it was a miserable time - watching myself diminish. Shutting up and taking the cheque was a shameful option for someone like me, but one I couldn't afford not to do.

When that stammering call came from the Managing Editor that I was to be 'considered for redundancy,' it threw me into an almost vomiting confusion. I was high as a kite one moment, seeing it as having my tether snapped to allow me to roam free again and find passion in my work. The next, plunged into the darkness – my four walls no longer viable, my debts called in, my car re-called.

Although I would have made myself redundant after crunching the numbers, I didn't realise, until much, much later, how it actually affected my soul, I suppose, as I watched working 'friends' disappear; e-mails cease to arrive in my box and calls go unanswered.

In newspapers one flicks and flits between friends, contacts and acquaintances. One walks a tightrope of what is acceptable to use and what isn't. With political friends – and I've had a good few – it's a ping-pong game of 'can I?' can't I?' Usually 'oh bugger it, I will.'

If the drip-fed 'confidence' worked to his or her advantage, there was a wink and a dinner wrapped in a warmth of friendship. If it went sour, it became a 'how could you?' a 'did you really think I meant that to come out?... and a long telephone silence, until you were needed again. Sometimes you'd simply run your course and were never needed again.

That was fine. That was acceptable. That was the game. It was the others, many close colleagues in fact, who disappointed me most. Cynical me could still, it turned out, be surprised and hurt by the shallowness of others – or should that be the opportunism of others – who wined and dined me when they thought I was useful or had the editor's ear. And disappeared when it was rather obvious I had neither his ear nor his regard.

At first the phone rang constantly. Journalists thrive on drama and misfortune - even their own. After saying how shocked, stunned and other variations on the theme, they all ended with more or less the same last words: 'Anyway, you'll be fine. Just look at the cash you made when you freelanced before. You'll get stacks of work.'

Some, in hindsight probably the more honest, didn't even bother to phone with false sorrow. Of course I always knew there were plenty who envied both my 'reported' salary and my apparent disdain for joining them at the office computers. But, it was still painful to be proved so right.

None of this frankly would really have bothered me even ten years earlier. It would be just another stage in the career. But being in one's 50s is to face the cul-de-sac, not the broad boulevard of job opportunities. (Even now I write in Mail features speak.)

And despite my jokes and banter at the farewell parties as I listened to more of the 'you'll be fine,' platitudes, my unfailing journalistic insight knew I probably wouldn't.

It didn't take long to realise that I couldn't earn – now that the accountants are in charge of all newspapers – even enough per month to cover my mortgage and my debts. Four months actually. And if I weren't to dwindle away the negotiated redundancy payment; the cashed-in early two pensions; then something radical had to be done.

Whether it was pride, or the realisation that I'd actually been bored rigid in both job and life for the past three years, I was not prepared to simply downsize my flat; cut my losses and scrabble in the freelance market for payments that at times were just an insult.

That first night of the redundo call, with two of my real friends and far too much red wine, ended with my dramatic announcement that I really was going to go to France. From that through all the negotiations, it was the only way forward.

In fact, after that, as I said, it all seemed so easy once the decision was taken and the movie started to play out in my head. To live a life in a perfumed cloud of wisteria and lavender; in a slow-motion muslin -wrapped fantasy where I would grow six inches (easy when you're half an inch over five feet) lose 20 years off my age and make a perfect omelette aux fines herbes.

In my mental meanderings over the years, usually fuelled

by red wine (French, of course) I saw myself languidly sashaying onto a terrace, platters of fresh figs and cheese in either hand, to add to the heaving plates of… more Frenchie things placed before my guests.

My friends, all beautiful and tanned, like I'd be, would look up and groan at more gorgeous things created by moi and I would shrug, gallicly and breathe 'c'est rien.' Behind them the swimming pool would shimmer into infinity, reflecting another perfect heat hazed day.

Really, I should have left it at that. An idea in my head - a daydream.

I can't, don't cook; frankly, despite the efforts of the TV masterchefs, not interested in trying. I've never made an omelette in my life. I loathe fines herbes. I don't even like the smell of lavender and what's wisteria? But the vision was too far gone to let go. Me and the dog - Thelma and Louise heading to the sunflowers.

During the summer of 2006 I wafted around Glasgow blithely telling everybody - taxi drivers, waiters, drunks in pubs - that I was off to live in the South of France. Yes, as soon as the flat is sold; one last great adventure - not a qualm in sight.

I made it into a great story and people envied me. They really did talk about 'living the dream' and how they planned to do it one day. I even started to believe it myself. It sounded pretty damned good.

And here I am. For the first time in my life I have a budget and a tight one at that. I have lived my life on a live for today, tomorrow we die basis, but suddenly tomorrow is almost here and I have to go where I can afford. It is a great shock to my flabby system. That means this crummy hotel.

The room has gone very cold now. I presume the radiator, which was barely warm when I arrived, has now been switched off entirely. The French sure know how to work to a budget. I cannot get the hang of it yet. I am starting though, to get the hang of this 'French thing.' It is not the France I thought I knew which of course was the France of a woman with a job, a regular income and a wallet bulging with credit cards. The France of exquisite châteaux hotels, private ski guides and spur of the moment week-ends in Paris.

This France is provincial, shuttered windowed France where, believe me, Frenchwomen DO get fat. It's not chic in any sense and at times driving at night through villages crouched around looming churches, it can feel almost threatening. So tonight in this tired, albeit spotless, hotel room, I have to take stock of the France I am now discovering.

There is no going back. I've become a victim of my own fantasy and big mouth. It's easier to go into the unknown than admit I can't hack it. Paradoxically I feel a long forgotten sense of glorious freedom.

It's a stomach-churning anticipatory excitement that I haven't felt in years. My life is no longer bound by work or child; my year no longer mapped out with familiar landmarks - my future no longer secure or safe.

And the man in the next room is either dead or has, like me, changed his habits and stopped snoring on every fifth wave. It no longer matters. Through the lace curtains the dawn is arriving. I can turn off the light and maybe sleep for an hour or two before facing a new day en France.

Chapter 3

I DIDN'T come straight to France from Glasgow. All didn't quite go to plan in selling my flat. The woman who'd agreed to buy it backed out at the last moment because her buyer had backed out. I'd already agreed to give her more time with her promises that she would complete very quickly. But time was running out. When she phoned me weeping, I was packing the last of my books into the cases. The removal men were due in three days and I'd booked for everything to go into storage, as there was no point in attempting to buy in France if I didn't know how much money I had.

I suppose at that point I could have stopped all this - decided this was meant to be and start looking for freelance work. Instead I listened to her promises to try and find another buyer and blatantly played on her conscience by pointing out that my flat would be packed up and empty in just a few days - all I possessed in a concrete warehouse. No one can sell an empty flat.

I continued packing, wondering what the hell I should

do. Good friends worried that I would rush into something unsuitable in France having, we thought, sold in Glasgow, had offered me a cottage on the Wiltshire/Dorset border from which I could flit back and forth cheaply to France. There they reasoned I could become acclimatised to a quieter existence and decide how much rural living I could take. I didn't intend to be there for more than a month so I gratefully accepted.

There was nothing for it. I had to move forward and pray my buyer would return. Four days later I was settled in the cottage, hurriedly furnished for me by my kind friends and peering out into the darkness of the country plucking up the courage to take Portia out on the lead to pee.

We both edged out into the night pushing to be last out. On the lane we stood frozen in fear. There were no stars, no moon and the few cottages behind us had lights so dim they could be candle-lit. Before us was a vast, dark tunnel of hedges and somewhere a cow mooed. We both shrieked. In the light of the industrial torch I was carrying, Portia looked back at me in mute plea: 'I'm a celebrity, get me out of here.' We turned and ran for home.

This did not augur well for life in La France Profonde. It was our nightly routine for what turned out to be the five months I was to live in the cottage, searching for houses on the internet at first, unable to think of doing anything about them. From the woman in Glasgow there was only silence and my old flat lay in unloved splendour. Barely a month into the new life, my son, Pierce broke his back in a motorbike accident and lay angry and sore in a Robocop body brace. From the day he broke the news to me that he'd bought a bike I had been fatalistically waiting for this to happen. This time he was lucky. He wasn't paralysed and he was alive. The bike, thank God was smashed beyond repair and for now at least he was promising he would never get another one.

With that and no word from my buyer I felt pretty adrift and unable to think about what was to come next. The redundancy cheque would not be paid in until April, but at least I had the cash from the early pension take-up along with two small pensions. And I had the column. But without the sale of the flat I could not move forward.

By day I took long walks with Portia on an ancient track above the estate where Madonna lived. I surprised myself by growing to enjoy the village and the neighbours whose growing friendship I appreciated. But I could not stay here forever and there was no going back.

By night I lay in bed conscious that without the dog I hadn't much reason to get up. And then, just when I thought I'd never hear her voice again, my buyer phoned to say she'd sold her house and mine was now back on. I fully expected her to offer a new, lower price, knowing she had me between a rock and a hard place. To her credit, she didn't and even moved her entry date forward to get the money to me quicker.

I could now start looking properly and arranged to visit more friends, Margaret and Bryan who had a newly renovated holiday house - a barn near Poitiers - to see if I liked their area. It was either that, or stick a pin in a map of France and go wherever it pricked. I got a £30 easyJet ticket and booked the blonde into kennels with a woman who sounded like the Queen. It was the start.

Her case for three nights was as heavy as mine, packed with the seven bottles of pills to counteract the allergies which, at their worst, can see her pull her hair out. A blood test has shown she's allergic to dust mites and fourteen types of grass. She also refuses to take the pills the normal way. The cost of her kennels at £92.50p for three nights is three times my flight fare. And I've packed pouches of her favourite food, which has to be arranged in a certain way on top of the dried food before she will eat anything.

The Queen gives me a condescending smile as I explain that the hysteric will only take her pills if squashed in cream cheese with wrap-around wafer thin ham. For almost a hundred quid I expect the ham to be organic and free range. I know as I leave she will prise her jaws open and shove them down her throat while reassuring me by phone that baby is having a great time.

I don't care. I hear her plaintive howl as I drive away and, although I care, I don't care. I don't even mind that it takes me nearly four hours to get to Stanstead and I am so late that I have to park in the short term car park at £24 a night!

I am on my way. I can smell the garlic and the Gaulloises. I feel liberated; hum a few bars of La Marseilles and order a snack pack (pate, cheese, biscuits) and a vin rouge, bien sûr, at a cost of almost £10 on board. I don't even bother that I'm in a middle seat with no pouch of mags in front of me. Actually there is no pouch. I can do this.

A few days later I am beginning to wonder. It starts with the language. I've heard it said that the only way to become really fluent in French is to have a French lover. Sadly, it was not an option on offer at the Alliance Française, in Glasgow's Park Circus last autumn.

In my two-week immersion course involving several hundred pounds and several hours a day, (lunch, full use of the library including DVDs, French only spoken) there was no small print offering that extra frisson of linguistic knowledge.

Which was probably why the very small, rather fat, actually very ugly Frenchman in dungarees, sitting at my friends' kitchen table, spluttered and blushed when I apparently propositioned him in front of his shocked wife.

Having delivered the stack of logs for the wood-burning stove, he'd been invited in for an aperitif to cement Scottish/French working relationships. That's how it's done in egalitarian France. He was met with a woman of a certain age, super-flushed with the earlier success of her accent in the market place. Parisienne? Non, Irlandaise, Écossaise.

A woman who tragically believed that speaking fast, flicking eyes and eyebrows, and doing a riff like Maurice Chevalier must mean she has total understanding of colloquial French. It worked like a dream - I was on a roll. My friends looked on , obviously with admiration and envy, as a I joked and laughed uproariously with the log man in the Charentois patois I'd grasped with amazing speed.

Well, okay, it worked for maybe ten minutes before I ran out of steam. But then, seeking common ground whilst making it plain I was a city gal(!), cue twitch of eyebrow, I asked him: Qu'est-ce que vous faites ce soir?'

I really just wanted to know where he and his wife and friends would spend Saturday night for fun - a restaurant, a bar, a party? Simple conversation to grasp the essence of local rural life. Unfortunately, I was still doing the Chevalier leer and Bardot pout. (Seriously, do the pout when speaking French… it really rounds the vowels.)

The wife's mono-brow hit her hairline as she shot me a look of horror combined with a definite tinge of disgust. He gulped his wine, flexed his dungaree straps, tugged the profuse hair peeking over his t-shirt, shot a glance at madame, reddened and finally looked at my brazenly smiling face to mutter:

'Je serais avec ma femme.' (I'll be with my wife.)

'At home?' I asked with, in hindsight, another Bardot come-hither smirk. 'All alone?' I have never known a Frenchman leave a drop of wine in his glass let alone half a glass. This one did. He sprinted - hard for a fat man - to the door with his wife close behind him giving me a last look of withering contempt.

It took me 24 hours to work out that it was all in the inflexion. That's the thing about French. Inflexion. Raise your voice at the wrong end of a sentence, or emphasise the wrong word and you could end up taking home a man in dungarees or tending to a black eye given to you by his wife.

That's why I cannot understand the number of people who move abroad without even a basic grasp of the language. Or, the number of people who have no intention of learning more than hello, goodbye and the bill, please.

Dordogne is full of them. Ex-pats, almost always English, speaking to other ex-pats in loud Home Counties voices. Quaffing cheap wine, their cheeks a spaghetti-junction of drink-broken veins, loudly proclaiming all that's wrong with Britain, they seem to take a perverse delight in only speaking their mother tongue to 'the frogs.'

And yes, when attempting to communicate with the

French they really do believe that shout loud enough and they will be understood.

They form little clubs to play golf or to fish, hold dinner parties of suburban naffness and loudly proclaim, within the safety of their own homes, all that's wrong with - France. If it weren't for the weather, they state with a sigh, looking homewards... Rubbish. None of them could afford to live in England any more, that's the simple truth. There they'd be just another big-mouth drunk in a semi wondering if they can afford the golf club fees this year.

In Dordogne, belly-up by the swimming pool they're masters of the Universe, last reminders of the men and women who conquered the world, creating an empire in the image of Bournemouth and Cheltenham. Is it any wonder that in vast tracts of France the English are quietly despised?

So, I may pick up the odd Frenchman when all I'm trying to ask is 'what do you do in the evenings around here?' Or even the odd black eye. But it will only be the inflexion that's wrong, not the language in which it's said.

In time the fluent French of my 20s will hopefully return. I haven't yet clicked back into effortless speech. The head starts throbbing after an hour and I'm still mentally translating instead of just being. I'm also using words like souliers for shoes instead of chaussures. 'The language of Molière,' guffawed my immersion teacher.

But hey, by at least trying, I made a man in blue dungarees very happy. It seems he returned alone a few days after I left, walking with a newly acquired stud swagger. My friends said he looked quite crestfallen when told the fast bit with the Bardot pout had left the building.

But the area was not for me I decided. Too north for the really hot weather I was seeking and because of the climate, too lush, and rather flat in parts although the villages were charming and it would have been nice to be near people I know.

Just an hour and a half away, Mary, my other great friend, has a holiday house in the Limousin where she and her husband spend most of the Summer, but apart from the flatness the reasons for not going there are exactly the same.

Returning from that first trip, it was a good job I didn't appreciate just how long I would continue shuttling back and forth.

Two weeks later I was heading for South West France and a tentative list of properties to see. Finding an even thinner Portia than the one I left and her pouches returned un-opened, I ditched the Queen and found a farmhouse kennels closer to home in which she was now happily, I hoped, being properly taken care of.

I'd decided to do the Midi-Pyrenees as I'd loved Toulouse on my one previous visit and liked the idea of being close to the Pink City. And now I was sitting in a Biarritz restaurant watching a very French spectacle unfold.

It was the waiter's overt attentiveness to the rather imperious middle-aged woman that first caught my eye. She'd disdained the first table offered with an eloquently raised laser groomed eyebrow.

Ushering her to a second, obviously more acceptable table, he settled her down with, for a French waiter, an almost obsequious display of devotion. My jaw dropped though as his head bobbed into her cleavage and appeared to kiss the tops of her breasts!

Good God I thought, have I driven to Italy in my headlong flight from the last two-star provincial hotel? But then, a tiny, wispy auburn-haired head peaked out from madame's bosom, and all became clear. His kiss was aimed for the upturned face of the sweetest little Yorkshire Terrier who was now tucked under madame's arm as she cluckingly undid her 'baby's' miniature parka, complete with fur hood.

Throughout the meal which followed – the ubiquitous foie-gras, breast of duck and what appeared to be a rather fine Brie – baby had her own little plate and punctuated each mouthful with a kiss for maman.

And all around them, other tables smiled and clucked back in return, or waved the paws of their own canine babes in salutation. No, I had not gone to some mad theme restaurant where dogs bring their owners. I was witnessing the French passion for pets.

There are few restaurants, hotels or even shops in France where dogs are not allowed; some restaurants will even bring a high-chair for the infant. As the Italians are to children, the French – that ordinarily most unsentimental of people – are to dogs.

Pets, pampered dogs that is, not the poor hunting dog chained for hours in the countryside, or the deserted dogs – too ugly, too big – who scavenge in every city.

These dogs are pretty miniatures; cute, groomed, beribboned, and often dressed, arm-candy – in the main, companions to a whole tranche of French women. I now firmly believe there is a generation of such women (mainly middle-aged) who have exchanged husbands for a four legged devotee who only asks food and water in return for life-long unconditional love.

Personally, I think it a more than fair exchange, but one does wonder what they have actually done with the men. Are they kept in kennels – tossed a chicken leg now and then? Or have they become house pets, too unruly to be taken out?

These women can be the wealthy, fur-coated Biarritz matrons who prowl Hermès, D & G and Armani, or the less obvious bourgeoisie in Toulouse and Paris, but all coo, cuddle and treat these dogs with an almost embarrassing demonstrative love.

Walking along the street with Fleurette or Albert, they suddenly stop, clutch the beast to their heart, shower it with kisses and murmured endearments before replacing it on the street and marching on.

As Frenchwomen can coldly, silently insult you with one languid sweep of the eyes, which price you from top to toe, it is a fascinating insight into their softer hearts. Or is it, as my embroidered cushion says: 'The more I see of men, the more I love my dog,'?

Traditionally such women have accepted their husbands' affairs (another enshrined national right in France) with sophisticated indifference. Perhaps though they have waited until now to get their revenge with a castrated bad-breathed pug who gazes at them from the other pillow.

My own companion, Louise to my Thelma, the hysterical Afghan, could be both a blessing and a problem in the months to come. I've always had Afghans in the belief that owners become like their dogs. Sadly, I'm the exception, having spectacularly failed over the years to become an anorexic, long-legged blonde – only mastering the blonde part, briefly the anorexic, but definitely the look of haughty disdain which hardly wins friends or influences people.

Now, when gravity yearly pulls me another inch closer to the ground, the difference is more marked and soon I'll be able to put a saddle on her and ride to town. She will make me friends, but I fear not in hotels and restaurants. It would be easier for her to sit me on her lap and clutch me to her bosom than the other way round. But these days I cannot think of many waiters who would swoop to kiss my sweet, upturned face.

So I watch the women and their well-behaved acolytes and visualise the chaos Portia would cause here with one sweep of her tail and a lunge for the Yorkie. It's time to return to the house search, somewhere sadly, rather more provincial.

Biarritz? An aberration. A brief interlude between yet another medieval village and lace-curtained lodgings. A longing for a bit of style and a walk along La Grande Plage in the hope that I'll be reinvigorated by the thundering waves and the back-drop of five-star luxury to return east and the next sweep of the Midi-Pyrenees.

A house or even a flat here? Only in my next incarnation, as a Gucci-wearing, snuffling pug, or preferably Yorkshire Terrier, condemned to a life of smother love between a matron's breasts. I think not….

But I do enjoy my night in the remarkably reasonable hotel bang on the beach-front and opposite the Casino; sleeping with the sound of the sea, opening the balcony to its sweet smell in the morning. I feel quite invigorated and decide to go have a look at Bordeaux.

It was sheer hubris of course. Having apparently overcome my previous spatial difficulties when driving on the right and with a good 1000 kms behind me now, I bowled along to Bordeaux with a song on my lips and joy in my heart.

Zipping in and out of the fast lane on the auto-route from Biarritz I felt at one for the first time with all the other drivers. Yes, I had clipped a pedestrian with the wing mirror again, but it was a slight tap in a ridiculously narrow street in Pau and unlike the woman in Cahors many years ago, he didn't even stumble, never mind fall.

So I wasn't particularly fazed on approaching Bordeaux even though it was massively larger than I'd realised. Even the converging auto-routes jammed with traffic didn't worry my newly-empowered self whose flat was sold.

And then the French threw me a googly. Tramlines, with hordes of bullet trams whizzing down the centre of the roads and along the Pont d'Aquitaine - the main route over the Garonne into the city centre. The last time I tangled with a tramline was in Blackpool riding my bike, aged 12. I still bear the scar on my ankle and the memory is not a good one.

At first I just felt mildly worried and tail-gated the other cars. But looming across the bridge was a demolition site stretching most of the riverbank. Major reconstruction was under way here with several temporary traffic lights, diversion signs with explanatory loops that were as clear as mud, all centred on a crazy roundabout.

Stay calm, keep breathing, follow the others, I thought. After all, I'd also been able to overcome my problems with roundabouts on this trip.

That problem reached its peak a few years ago in Lausanne outside the Olympic HQ which is accessed off, as far as I'm concerned anyway, the world's busiest and biggest roundabout. Even now I don't really want to discuss it in any detail. It's enough to say that after 40 minutes circling - cut-up by coaches, cars and bikers - my magic roundabout whirl was stopped by a Swiss policeman who'd been watching the performance from his sentry-box.

It involved my total mortification, piercing whistles, two of his colleagues, hand-signals and the total cessation of all traffic except me. Okay?

So when I found myself first car at the first red light in front of the tramlines criss-crossing the end of the bridge I knew I was in trouble. Real trouble when all the cars behind started hitting the horns even though the light was red. Now I know that in France you can turn on some red lights, but I was going straight across - in front of the trams on to the roundabout. As the noise grew to a crescendo I decided death by tram was preferable to a lynching and hit the pedal.

I was in no state to read the loops or face another red light so I did a neat circle and ended up back on the bridge going the other way. By now, mildly hyperventilating, I re-crossed, swung round and on to the other side in the manner of a show-jumper who's had a refusal and turns back into the fence.

What do you think the odds are for being the first car again at the first red traffic lights? In all I went over the bloody bridge five times before finally making a dash for the narrow back streets. The trail of fag ash down my jumper was a clear indication of the stress I was under, but I kept going, bouncing along the cobbles, both wing-mirrors now flattened to the sides of the Megane. I didn't bother to look for felled pedestrians – you get blasé after the first two.

Suddenly there was a broad, real street in front of me. Unfortunately there was no right turn and surprise, surprise, I turned left and onto a one-way system leading me... yes, back over the bridge.

Several years ago, overcome with vertigo on the terrifying, single-track coast road of Slea Head, in the Dingle Peninsula and faced with a bus load of American tourists, I simply stopped the car and threw the keys at the coach driver. Reverse? At 5mph I'd laboured, hugging the cliff, to get three quarters of the way up and almost made it to the bend so I'm afraid reversing was not an option.

Every screeching nerve in my body begged me to do the same now. Get out, walk away... stuff the traffic and the trams, stuff Bordeaux... just sod them all. The red mist had descended. Don't mess with me. I'm a woman on the edge.

As I was locked into another traffic jam I was stopped anyway. Gradually brain and body re-engaged and I pulled back from the brink. Reason prevailed, helped by the auto-route sign pointing to Albi.Birthplace of Toulouse Lautrec - small person with attitude and an Absinthe problem. Sounds like my kind of town.

Chapter 4

IN the film Falling Down, Michael Douglas went off his head in backed-up traffic heading to LA. Yesterday, I was a woman on the edge in Bordeaux after several trips over the Garonne bridge. Fortunately I did not have a gun, but I have the ultimate respect for what he did.

Today, I am a very calm, slightly Audrey Hepburnish (in my dreams), rather mysterious woman sitting at an enormous linen swathed table in a restaurant across from the cathedral of Sainte Cecille, in Albi.

There is no one else in the wood-panelled dining room, but the sun is shining on the impeccably clean silver and glassware and I have navigated a very simple ring-road to get here. Three very ordinary roundabouts and a few blue signs to the centre. This is definitely my kind of 'lively city' as given to the estate agents.

It would be rude to think of boring budgets in a place like this. My mouth takes over and asks for a 'coup de champagne.' It is not really expensive here and I have been very stressed after Bordeaux… I deserve it.

I order half a dozen escargots, lamb cutlets and a little - OK, in truth, large - glass of local red and hit my mobile. I phone my son, my friends and give a description and price of all that's going into my mouth and how I really think this could be it.

In this setting I believe in France again and where I'm going and why. I hum French songs to myself, watch the light hit the cathedral and visualise taking pals here in high summer. I imagine myself being warmly welcomed by the owner who ushers us to 'my' special table and suggests a few little morsels kept for his favourite customers.

I will laugh merrily and in perfect French chide him for being absent last week when I brought a table of ten. He will feign desolation and - this is when I ask myself - what the hell are you doing? Face the truth. You only love France when it is perfect and you can't afford perfect any more. You shouldn't even be sitting here drinking champagne. Those days are gone, gone.

Travelling alone is to have a non-stop conversation with yourself in your head. You go on and on and can't tell yourself to shut the hell up for an hour or so. So I turn off the mobile with a sigh and listen. It's an endless stream of questions.

Why have you spent almost six days, driven 1300 km, sat with three estate agents and not once crossed the threshold of any house for sale? Why have you net-trawled hundreds, possibly thousands, of houses in the past three months and not once arranged to cross the threshold of any house for sale?

Why have you now been to France five times recently, haemorrhaging cash every time, ticking off whole areas based on the colour of the roof tiles? At this rate you'd better ask The Herald editor to change your column from French Leave to The Long Goodbye!

They are fair questions I concede. And I have to admit that there is a major problem at the heart of all this. It is hard to change the ingrained habits of a lifetime and work to a fixed price. I do not really like the houses I can afford – it is that simple, that pathetic. All the houses I want to see are at least 40,000 euros over my limit. I could do it, but I would be left without a sou to fall back on.

And if no freelance work comes my way to augment the two pensions I cashed in early, then I'm well and truly buggered. I am a rather reckless woman who has survived many cash crises by the skin of her teeth and rarely compromised, but even I can see I cannot go on like that.

Ah, but there is something terribly tempting about going for broke and trusting in luck that something will turn up. After all it always has in the past. Why shouldn't it in the future?

I feel immensely cheered and optimistic after that little chat. And we, myself and I, have agreed on one important thing apart from starting to religiously do the lottery.

This is where I want to be, somewhere in the triangle of Toulouse, Montauban and Albi - I like the red tiles.

Well, I'm pretty certain this is where I want to be, although I still have a hankering to check out the towns around La Rochelle on the West Coast and around Burgundy could be interesting. But if I do that when will it all end, never mind where? No, enough, I'll go home, make some firm arrangements and return with full concentration.

And, feeling very grown up, I promise myself to look at my price range - initially. But I will also look above my range. After all, everybody knows that you can usually knock 20 per cent off French house prices, sometimes more. It would be foolish to miss a bargain just because I think I couldn't afford it, wouldn't it?

I smile warmly at the hovering waiter who rushes to light my cigarette. Another glass of champagne perhaps, madame? Oh, go on then... after all, it's been a very productive lunch.

This glow of decision lasts until the third night back in England and another fruitless trawl on the internet, even though I am now confining my search to more or less one area. And there are no more excuses left.

Portia is back to full health having bizarrely started to overcome her allergy to the countryside and her forced removal from Glasgow. Her hunger strike is over and she's no longer ripping her hair out. Missives were finally completed on my flat and the cash is in the bank account. There is nothing stopping me now from buying in France.

So why have I re-started the 3am panic attacks? Why do all of the houses sent to me appeal so little? They're all, more or less, exactly what I specified. Old, exposed stone, fireplaces and wood-burners, rooms big enough to take my 3,000 plus 'library,' with swimming pool or enough ground to have one. They're all instantly habitable because, although in theory I love the idea of converting some massive old barn, in practice I'm aware than I can barely paint my nails.

And they're all available for the price of a two-bedroom flat in the less desirable parts of Glasgow. So why am I not opening the champagne and singing Non, je ne regrette rien?

I am not being helped by my son, whose enforced home confinement gives him more time to telephone torment his mother. 'If you go anywhere in the country, you'll be a mad old lush in 12 months,' he says blithely.

'I'm a mad old lush now,' I counter, 'thanks to you.'

'Everyone says you're off your head if you buy without renting first,' he continues. 'You'll buy something, hate the area and you won't be able to sell. Houses in France can take years to sell. And you know you hate the country and you'll be too scared to go to bed. You're a wreck now and you're still in the English countryside. What'll you be like in the French?'

'An even madder old lush obviously,' I reply, adding: 'I'm hanging up now.'

Actually he hit the nail on the head. Of course I know why I'm waking up in a cold sweat and gazing lovingly at the brochure for my now 'sold' flat, stroking the pictures.

One look through the bedroom window of this pretty cottage tells me instantly - it's pitch bloody black with cow shapes moving on the hillside. There's not even a glow from a nearby town, 'cos there isn't a nearby town.

I haven't had a pair of heels on in weeks; my hair once lovingly tended by Taylor Ferguson now resembles the thatched cottages in this village and I pull on the same jumper and trousers day after day. I don't even put make-up on any more!

I've stopped lighting the fire because I'm fed up dragging logs in just to watch them burn and I've taken to hanging by the door to catch the postman for a quick chat. And I've even started drinking Bovril, for goodness sake.

Yesterday I got very over-excited because a well-dressed elderly man knocked on my door, tipped his deer-stalker hat and invited me to a meeting to discuss the village fête to be held in June.

So over-excited that it took me until the twelfth telephone call to friends in Glasgow to realise they weren't sharing my enthusiasm. In fact, most were asking if I were perhaps a little bit depressed?

Planning a village fete? Is this what I have come to? Even worse will I be desperate if not asked to do the same in France? The friends who gave me this cottage as a foretaste of rural life were very wise. If I'm miserable here in a village of well-heeled, cultured mostly London retirees, what will I be like in a hamlet of insular French farmers?

To an extent I've been blinded by the vision of the terrace, the table, the glowing tanned friends gathered at the height of summer to toast my much younger, taller self. Blinded by the vision of me and the Afghan running in slow-motion through the sunflowers; blinded by the insane belief that I will suddenly go to market and overthrow a lifetime of ready-made meals and restaurant reservations.

Now, thanks son, I peer into the future and see a mad old lush with black roots, clutching a telephone and babbling incoherently to all back home who are still listening. Or is that my present?

So I have re-instructed the estate agents. I must, must be on the edge of a lively village. One with people who go out after dark and with at least three restaurants; it must have street lights and be no more than thirty minutes away from a big city.

No hamlets, no houses with woods attached, nothing described as 'peaceful' or 'remote, but not isolated.' The area must have broadband and a fast road to the nearest airport.

There absolutely has to be room for a pool… I refuse to compromise on that vision.

In a week's time I leave again for Toulouse and a week of very serious searching. Winter is a good time to house-hunt – you can count the people who come out once the light goes, or not.

Sadly, being away means I will not make the meeting for the planning of the village fête. I'm strangely disappointed as I think I have some rather good ideas. My friends were right - perhaps I am just a little depressed. Being a mad old lush is a far better idea.

My new-found equilibrium is somewhat disturbed by a strange phone call just before I left. The booming voice of a man garbled that a mutual friend in Province told him I was looking for a house in the Languedoc.

In fact I'd discounted the area long ago, but before I could say no - too dear, too many scorpions and as I'd discovered, in an earthquake zone - he launched into a heartfelt tirade against estate agents.

The gist of it was that virtually all French ones were lying, double-dealing , unprofessional crooks. Even worse were the English ones who would rip you off twice by adding on their fee to the French fee when all they'd done was ring round other agents in the area.

House prices, he warned, were a moveable feast depending on how the viewer was perceived, as were their fees.

'Turn up in an expensive car looking rich and another €50,000 has gone on to the price before you've even got through the door.

'Pay the asking price and you may as well have mug stamped right through you. Go in 30 per cent under, but expect to settle around 20 per cent. The minute he says he'll put your offer to the sellers you know you've hit the true price.

'Never, ever believe that the charming little man in the rumpled shirt escorting you round all these houses really cares about you. He's an actor. An actor!'

When he paused for breath after what seemed an eternity, I tentatively asked: 'I'm sorry, who is this?' It barely put him off. He muttered a name and the name of our mutual friend, and continued his monologue, which frankly, can't be repeated as his denunciation of the entire profession became increasingly scurrilous.

It was nothing personal he added. Even if he'd paid a staggering 15 per cent agent's fees in buying his last house, his fifth in 25 years of living in France. It was fact - they're all bastards.

There is some, some, tiny truth in what he says. The French themselves are not quite sure of estate agents. Only 50 per cent of houses sold are via an agency. Private or notaire sales are far more popular.

There is no fee regulation, but one can expect to pay anything between five and eight per cent – the house price says fees included, but make no mistake, the buyer is paying. Add to that the notaire's fee for drawing up the buying agreement and another eight to ten per cent is clocked up.

There is also the curious French habit of placing their

houses with several estate agents, all showing a different price. It's your tough luck if you pick the one showing the dearest.

For me though, the most unsettling part of dealing with agents so far is their apparent reluctance to actually show you a house. In fact, their determination to almost prevent you from seeing any house on their books.

Don't expect to walk off the street and maybe, possibly, arrange to see a house from their window display that you might just want to buy. Dear me no – no appointment, no chance. You've come in here to buy a house? How weird is that?

If you persist you may be able to wrest a book of properties from the unwilling hands of the receptionist just to have a look at what they have, but don't dare ask a question without an appointment. And when you finally are awarded the privilege of sitting opposite a live agent, be specific, be very specific.

One couple who thought they'd covered everything in their wish list - remote country house, no neighbours, good views, away from traffic - were driven to what they were assured was exactly as specified. The house as it came into view was perfect. The nuclear power station sited two fields away was not.

The agent just shrugged: 'But you never said anything about nuclear power stations.' At the next agent's they revised the list to include no nuclear power stations, (of which there are quite a few in France) and added in sewage treatment plants and abattoirs just for luck.

Again they were taken to the 'perfect' house. Unfortunately, in the pretty grounds conversation was all but impossible. The main auto-route south whizzed by practically at the back gate. 'But you never said anything about auto-routes,' shouted the agent.

I believe they settled on an apartment in Bournemouth.

This week I have appointments with four different agencies in my preferred triangle of Albi, Toulouse, Montauban. They have e-mailed me with times, directions, places to stay in the area and a selection of houses - none of which fulfil my requirements, despite lengthy telephone conversations.

And they have all, all, made it very clear that if I intend to cancel, be late, change the arrangement I must let them know well in advance. These days I know what they're really saying is: 'If you must insist on us showing you houses, and we've bothered to arrange some, don't mess with us. We have far better things to do then screw up our day taking you places.'

Anyway, back to the man on the phone. 'Remember too that most rural French are dolts – straw in the ears. Find some like-minded souls before you settle anywhere. Non-French. Don't renovate. No one wants to work here, you'll be left in a cloud of dust and the locals will rip you off even more than the estate agents.

'Food is fine, but you'll get bored with it. You'll get to the stage where if you get another plate of bloody foie gras and onion confît, you'll throw the bloody thing at the hostess. Get a pool or no-one will come out to visit you.

'And be careful you don't get field syndrome? Field syndrome? That's when you stand outside your lovely house in a large French field and think: 'what the f**k am I doing here?'

I manage to interject with a weak: 'So you're advising against?'

'God no, wouldn't live anywhere else,' he replied.

I had reason to remember his advice as once again I was sitting in yet another agent's car on my way to see houses, which did not remotely fit the ones we'd discussed on the phone. She was English, well groomed and well-manicured, but the car was a rust bucket of an ancient Peugeot. Which in one way was good, as there would be no problem with my smoking. Anyway, since almost half the agency's brochures were already under my feet in the passenger seat along with sweet papers, a bit of ash wouldn't make much difference.

She'd whisked me so fast out of the office in the pretty town where Charlotte Grey was filmed that I was still reading the details of the houses rather than looking at where we were going. When I did, I wished I hadn't.

It could have been Rannoch Moor in the desolate Highlands of Scotland. Bleak moorland stretching out as far as one could see. Bleak that is, apart from the Nissen huts, the barbed wire and the numerous warning and keep out signs.

'I know,' said the estate agent with a sly sideways glance, 'This bit isn't quite so pretty. It's where the French Army come on manoeuvres.' Pause.' Have you seen them in uniform? Incroyable!'

Given that we'd already spiralled up twisting roads with vertiginous drops, after emerging out of the oppressive Avyeron Gorge, and were 100 km north from where I had asked to be taken, I was in grudging awe of her abilities to both understate and titillate.

Twenty minutes further on and the thought of the French equivalent of the SAS parachuting in and commandeering my remote farmhouse was strangely compelling, engendering fantasies too disgraceful to admit to even here.

My khaki daydream ended abruptly. We had arrived at the 'edge of village, not too remote, great grounds, character property.' I presumed we had parked in front of a 'dependance,' or outbuilding. Silly me – this was the house.

I helped hold on to the rotten barn doors in front of the sliding windows at presumably the best bit of the house as she pushed from inside. The light revealed a small white room with a central fireplace, mezzanine floor which appeared to have a four-poster bed and a galley kitchen at which even slaves would turn up their noses.

In my head Amy Winehouse's refrain:'I don't want no rehab... no, no, no' was pulsating. It was to become the backbeat to this trip and now possibly to my life.

'No, no, no,' I told her refusing to go beyond the alleged three bedrooms. 'At least look at the garden,' she coaxed. Garden? What Garden? There was a big, overgrown chunk of land looking up to the church (cemetery over the wall?) and a few slabs denoting the terrace. 'Imagine,' she said waving to a lumpy far corner. 'The pool, the night sky...' (Yeah, the drone of helicopters, the trundle of tanks.... waves of soldiers running up the road.)

God she was good, bless her. But not that good, not at almost £200,000. Way, way over budget anyway. 'No, no, no.'

Passing through the admittedly stunning 'plus beaux

villages de France,' Najac, we then moved on. She was beginning to take on board the fact that I did not want to be up this high, had vertigo problems and actually didn't want this area ever, ever. All already specified in the several chats with her office.

But, as she pointed out, I was booked for the night in Saint Antonin Noble Val (more on THAT later) and might as well go with the flow. To be fair, one house, despite its rather ugly stone exterior had rather appealed. It was a former convent, now 90 per cent converted into a four-bedroomed village house with courtyard and land just to the side. I'd always threatened my school nuns that I'd have a late vocation, so there was a perverse attraction.

Where do I begin? Cleverly cut out of the advert's picture was the former school next door, boarded and wired up and bang in your face. The lovingly converted ground floor combination kitchen, dining room, sitting room was - once in - not too bad.

But as we left the warmth and the scent of desperation from the young English owner married to the much older man, the cold permeated even on this fine day. The money had obviously run out beyond this point and what was left was the decaying memory of a house of women with little warmth in their hearts. As a convent girl from the age of two and a half, I can say this - even while paying tribute to the many wonderful teachers I knew. There were also some very, very bad ones.

Now, I've not mentioned my psychic abilities so far. (So, please keep a checklist - spatial problems, vertigo, claustrophobia, fear of the dark etc., etc.) Anyway, at this stage all you need to know is that I can sense a house and its past inhabitants within seconds. I feel dead people.

By the 'salon' and the first bedroom I was ready to run. Hackles rising. 'No, no, no.' The estate agent again, bless her, said let's keep going just for the girl downstairs. Of course, I am polite. By the second floor and the glimpses into the sadly semi-furnished rooms and a coldness far beyond lack of heating, politeness no longer came into it. Out, now.

Driving away I asked the estate agent if she hadn't felt something. She shrugged and said the upper rooms weren't used that often. Fifteen minutes further on, she pointed out a house just off the road in the trees. She said she didn't know why but it just felt 'horrible' inside and they couldn't sell it at any price.

'There are lots of crucifixes on every wall. Horseshoes on the stairs. Really odd.'

Really?

Tired, I let my head drop and had another daydream of waves of French soldiers powering off the moor and seeking rescue. It's amazing how you can find the best in any situation.

'No, no, no.'

That night - I suppose it was about 11pm - I was hanging out of my bedroom window in St Antonin Noble Val, hiding the red end of my fag with my hand and blowing smoke as far away as I could from my large room and muslin clad four poster in the upmarket chambre d'hôte.

Earlier, huffing and puffing, climbing the two flights of stairs to my room I'd merrily told the Dutch owner (married to a German) 'that's what smoking does.' She just smiled. Unfortunately I expressed my delight too quickly at the lovely bedroom and its carefully-chosen antiques dappled in sunlight, so I had no get-out when she smiled again, adding: 'This is a no-smoking house.'

After the day I've had I'm ready to fling myself on the bed, kick my legs, bite the sheet, roll around and yell: 'S'not fair.' But I don't, because I'm a middle-aged woman and the appropriate response to such a temper tantrum would be to section me.

So I reply calmly 'not a problem,' and fling myself on the bed groaning and rolling the second she leaves.

Now I was back in the room after yet another fruitless day with yet another estate agent in an area of no interest, miles from where I wanted to be, which had ended with her and me sinking a couple of red wines and shaking our heads.

And of course I was smoking. You really think you get a pristine bedroom just because of a red cross on a cigarette?

Anyway, St Antonin Noble Val is, of course, very beautiful, with winding lanes that have the feel of Venice. But it's in the Avyeron Gorge, which should have given me a clue. To get there you drive through tunnels cut under the cliffs, weave up and down and often share the road with wild mountain goats. Apparently, given the vertigo problem, I was lucky in that I'd happened upon the low road and not climbed up, to subsequently plummet down, 'the pretty road.' Praise the Lord.

And now looming in front of me as I puffed away was the cliff - overwhelming, overpowering and over there. In the light of the moon I could see into the gardens of the ancient houses and their not so ancient rubbish. In the awful silence a cat caterwauled and the shock made me start back knocking the red tip off the cigarette.

There was no conflagration, thank God, given the time of the year, so I lit another one and pondered the stars, the cliff and more of that shuddering silence, which seems to be following me around. Of course, I could understand the magic of it all and see how it would entrance the weary and the soul-seekers. And the bloody nuts.

It just plunged me into thoughts of death and the clichéd acceptance of the unblinking indifference of the Universe. And, you've guessed, there was no mini-bar to lift my spirits to the point where I could weave out of the window and throw kisses to the twinkling stars.

The next morning at breakfast, the refectory table was shared with an English couple and an English man. The German owner, unlocking the French multi-padlocked windows to allow me into the garden for my 'first' smoke, spoke, of course, perfect English. I subsequently discovered that 20 per cent of the local population were English, and that there was a growing resentment in the area over their 'snobbishness.'

Anyway, the breakfast club's distaste of my nicotine need was palpable and so I heartily launched into a friends-making exercise. 'My God,' I told them. 'Wasn't that terrifyingly silent last night? And the cliff? Wooooooh.'

'Each to their own,' said Mrs (sensible shoes, no make-up, buttering her chunk of bread and slathering it with honey) Short-bobbed hair. Her self-satisfied smile at her husband and the other man (all my age) made me want to sock her.

I just laughed, deliberately choosing a banana even though I wanted to slather honey on a chunk of bread. 'House-hunting?' I asked.

'Yes,' she replied with a smug glance. 'We have houses in

Spain and London and thought we'd look here as an extra.'

And you? I direct the question to the bored-looking - but I have to say, rather wealthy looking - other man. 'I have houses in several countries,' he answered, trying to look humble, but failing miserably. 'I've just sold here because my wife didn't like it. Too big and too remote. She just never wanted to be here. You?'

I act as if I'm trying to measure my words, casting a look at Mrs Shortbob. 'Well, yes,' I say, drawing out the yes. 'Unfortunately, the silence is too much for me here and frankly, the houses are far too small.'

'I have an enormous library and a number of paintings, so it seems I'm destined for the rather boring option of a château. I'd hoped for a more simple country house. It's a pity I suppose that I can't find one.

'But definitely not here anyway, too many English, but then...'at this I raise my eyebrows and look at Mrs Shortbob, 'Each to their own.'

Chapter 5

DEAR God, I promise I will never, ever, complain again about the occasional misery of solitary driving and travelling. I swear I will never, ever, wish for a companion to share my seemingly endless search for that perfect house at the end of the rainbow.

The reason for this heartfelt prayer is sitting opposite me - a broad shouldered 6ft 2ins tall blond. Classically good looking in that sulky, spoilt, flicked, discontented English public schoolboy way, he is studying the wine list in the restaurant.

Naturally it is the dearest restaurant in this part of the Tarn and Garonne. He can sniff them out wherever we end up. Tentatively I suggest a pichet of the local – and 'extremely good' I add – red. He looks at me as if I'd suggested quaffing the stomach acid of a gout-ridden goat and languidly orders a bottle costing twice what I'd normally pay if pushing the boat out in Britain.

He speaks little French but can speed read a wine-list like a Sorbonne professor on an expense account. Of course I know he will disdain the fabulous (all relative) value of the set menu and latch onto the priciest items on the a la carte because 'it's the only thing I like.'

If I demur, he'll sigh, shuffle in his seat, slap the menu on the table and say: 'Fine. Then I won't eat. There's no point because there's nothing else I want. You just carry on.'

I also know that by the end of the meal we'll be hissing and spitting like a couple meeting for a 'civilised' pre-divorce settlement. My face will have moulded itself into a Churchillian maw of distaste and defiance - a martyr's visage. His will be cold, bored and irritable.

I'll sigh heavily, staring at a corner of the high ceiling; then abruptly push my chair from the table to go and stand outside in the cold night air, puffing a fag, feeling sorry for myself, glaring at his expensively clothed tweed back through the window.

And I know, as usual, that I will be paying for the privilege.

So why, why do I persist in believing that travelling with my son could be a joyous, life-enhancing experience? One that might leave me bathed in the warmth of his love and concern?

After all, I am no novice to this. From the age of seven (he is now 25) we have travelled the world in a whirlwind of mutinous silences and huffs, accompanied by screams from me that I will never be conned again; will never, never, go anywhere abroad with him ever, ever again. Anywhere, actually, ever, ever again.

We have sat glowering at each other, exhausted by our verbal onslaughts, in some of the most glorious spots on the planet - the Maldives, Thailand, Marrakech, the French

Alps, the Hamptons, Cape Cod to name but a handful.

I remember in particular, the beach at Beau Vallon, in the Seychelles – a restaurant beside a pool peppered with underwater lights, the phosphorescent surf swooshing just beyond the flaming torches lit by gentle smiling staff as the sun set.

They were still there, hovering silently in the shadows as like two heavyweight boxers we sat in our corners eyeing each other up before the next bout. There was no-one else left in the restaurant, or in the sand-floored bar which melded into the softly-lit, fully-manned reception. It was 9pm.

I had failed miserably again, picking an hotel filled with honeymooners - and us. In their individual beachside luxurious imitations of cabanas – outside showers in Zen gardens, rose petals strewn over pillows under teak four-posters, DVD players, spa menus. They were already, well, fast asleep - or something.

Perhaps they were lying watching the moon, listening to the surf in their hammocks strung between the palm trees on their private bits of beach. In this little bit of paradise we had all this too, plus an extra four-poster – a veritable suite as the noughts on my credit card confirmed.

A four-piece band in the corner of the open dining room played gamely on into a fast little Motown set that begged for my sinuous moves. I'm a good dancer, if sometimes a touch too Suzi Quatro – with bouncing head and shrugging shoulders – maybe a few, just a few, too many pouty twirls and side-slides depending on how much red.

But, that summer he was 15 and a half and, I have to say, I was looking pretty good. (Hollywood types would have had 'lipo,' I'd had a gall bladder operation. A no-fat diet to minimise the pain pre-op had shifted the few stones of blubber I'd acquired over the previous few years.) I couldn't pinch an inch and would have licked myself if I'd been chocolate.

Added to my bliss was my totally single state. His father and I had finally given up the ghost after 18 years. He had been working in London all week, me in Glasgow. When I realised I preferred Friday night's Coronation Street to the sound of his key in the door, I knew it was time to go. Or rather, it was time he went. I'm sure he knew it too when he looked at the overweight, overpaid sloth on the sofa.

Anyway, that holiday. Back home I had a new gorgeous Georgian conversion that was all mine – every piece, every fabric chosen solely by me – no compromising required, no committee meetings, no memos on the fridge.

I was responsible for nothing and no one. Correction. Responsible for me and the tanned, cold blue-eyed blond sitting opposite. And he was as mysterious to me as perhaps I ultimately was to his father. I was tanned too, blonde too, and mildly, just mildly anorexic, enjoying the fact that my shoulder blades were clearly visible for the first time in years; determined they would stay that way as I calorie-counted through my new life.

'Five quid,' I'd offered in a wheedling, whining tone.

'No,' came the curt reply.

'A tenner for just one.'

'No.'

'A tenner, unlimited jet-ski use for the rest of the holiday and a packet of fags thrown in for good measure.'

'No,' he spat nastily. 'I don't even bloody smoke.'

'Right. I'll get you into the casino and teach you how to play craps.' It was my best, and last shot, forlorn and resigned, and he didn't need to be Poirot to sense it. He put his face inches from mine.

'I will not, repeat not, dance with you. Got it?'

'Why not? There's no bugger here but the band. No one will see you. Go on. You just have to stand there. I'm on holiday too.'

'No, no and no. They'll think I'm your toy-boy.'

'Toy-boy? Toy-boy?' I looked at him and tried not to laugh. 'Do you honestly think that anyone could seriously believe that? Jesus. The way we've been arguing they'd bloody know that if you were my toy-boy you'd have been sacked, fired, stuck on the next plane home. Gone. Vamoosed. Told to sod bloody off.'

He raised an eyebrow. Gave me the evil eye. Out of the shadows a sensitive five-star waiter glided over to re-fill my empty glass. Automatically I totted up the calories. Seafood didn't count, so okay there. White wine didn't really either – it's basically water, isn't it? So I was probably around my daily stay-thin 500 calories. Okay, now and again, 750 calories.

The waiter glided away as discreetly as he'd arrived. Pierce and I renewed our vicious eye contact - our 'waiter' smiles erased. Oh to hell, I decided, kicking off my heels, heading determinedly and alone for the dance floor.

'Mum, mum,' hissed the boy. 'What are you doing now?'

'Dancing,' I threw back as I shimmied on to 'Tears of a Clown.'

I felt, rather than heard on the soft sand, his mortified exit. And not for the first, and certainly not for the last time, I wondered why I continued to travel with him.

We can't even make the airport in companionable pleasure. By the time the flight is called he's on one side of the departure lounge and I'm on the other. With a face you'd leave well alone. But like Frankenstein and his monster, there are moments when, convulsed with laughter and love, there is no one else I would rather be with. This is not one of them. So why are we here?

Basically he has conned me into it again, because he knows I'm desperate to show him the area of France I'm now convinced is for me. The roles are reversed in our relationship. I seek his approval – something I've never done from any man. If he approves, I'm happy. If he doesn't, then he's a spoilt brat who knows bugger all.

When he broke his back, of course he returned to work far too early before any real healing and ultimately he had to accept his doctor's orders for a cocktail of painkillers and time off.

So, sun and a change of scene were called for. He would join me on my house search in France. I'd pulled the plug on his suggestion that the two of us would head for a ridiculously expensive holiday in the Indian Ocean which he claimed he would go 'halfers on.' I know where Pierce is concerned I'm buttoned up the back, but even I'm not that stupid.

Of course I was that stupid - again. 'Halfers' didn't apply to France apparently – some small print in a son's agenda – but it took a day to discover that, after I'd forked out for flights and hire car. (And of course, with regard to said car, despite having driven thousands upon thousands of kilometres around France I am incapable of even sitting behind a wheel apparently, so he took over.)

A part of me, given my spatial and roundabout problems, was quietly relieved. It's why on my solo trips I often envied the ease of being a mere wife, but not a mother. So, I clung to the handrest, warning that I would vomit if he didn't slow down.

Of course saying so only engendered a madness - a 'yee-hah' as we overtook even the fastest of the fast. The throbbing pain over the left eyebrow which I associate with travels with my son - which had begun almost immediately - was now intense.

By the time we arrived in Moissac to 'Le Moulin' on the banks of the Garonne, I was fast losing the will to live - anywhere. Surprisingly after a swift appraisal of the hotel and our room with its wrought-iron balcony overlooking the lazy length of the river, he decided he rather liked it.

The throbbing lessened…

Back in the restaurant, the wine had arrived. 'You shouldn't drink with those pills,' I warned, to be given a look, which tells me to know my place. Three glasses in I was glad he did, as he directed a beatific smile my way.

'I think you've made the right choice,' he said, mellowed by the combination of a grand cru and super plus codeine.

'I really like this area and I love Moissac. Great feel, good restaurants. This is actually the perfect place. Toulouse 40 minutes away, ski-ing an hour-and-a-half, the Med just two hours. Biarritz, Barcelona, Paris…' he gestured in the distance with a lazy wave.

The throbbing had virtually ceased. Pathetically grateful for his interest (finally) and a chance for one of our rare 'good' evenings, I leaned forward smiling, nodding him to continue in his expansive mood.

'So. Stone. Toulousean red brick. Terraces of course, plenty of land, ideally out in the country. I could get a dog and keep it here for when I come over. You'll need at least three bedrooms, preferably four, and no-one must use mine.'

Yes,' he concluded – charm playing across his features, raising his glass to me. 'Very good choice.'

Had he been any man other than my son I would have slapped the patronising shit and called a taxi. Instead, yet again I nodded him onwards.

'Now all we have to do is find this house,' he added, adopting a world weary wisdom. (God, were my hands ever itching.)

'Mind you, it will be hard at your price if what you've seen so far is anything to go by.'

I nod again, lulled (conned) by the warmth and enthusiasm in his voice, replying with a sophisticated laugh: 'Yep. Actually, in truth, what I really need is a rich man,' I drawl, with a world-weary, actually fag weary cough.

For a moment we're as one. We agree a title would be preferable; a widower with no children so that Pierce would inherit the château, the Paris apartment, the Provençal mas, the bijou Belgravia pied a terre. Oh, how we laugh.

But as ever the laughter stops and Pierce peers at the

dregs of his glass as he listens to my prattle. Eventually a look of incredulity crosses his face.

It's the moment the out-of-towners walk into the local bar. The jukebox – if there'd been one – would scratch to a halt; a glass would shatter from the hand of the old timer at the counter, and all eyes would turn to... moi.

He has loudly uttered the words. 'Let's be serious here mum. What do you have to offer a man? Come on...really?' The throb slowly begins to pulse again as I watch him eating and sipping his crème brûlée and armagnac, fussily brushing crumbs from the damask-draped table.

I'm conscious of the French glancing at us and wondering who we are, why we're here out of season and why we are in conflict.

'Actually, Pierce, you're right,' I say with a tight grin. 'I have absolutely nothing, nothing to offer a man. Not even my black American Express credit card.'

He only looks up as I stand up; head held high; fag clutched ready to light. He's still looking as I leave the restaurant telling the girl at the desk: 'My son will be paying.'

By the time he catches me up on the little bridge crossing the Canal du Midi, we've each independently decided to start again, again and discuss our plans for the next few days.

Come morning we're sitting in the impeccable silver Mercedes belonging to Jean-Louis, the Moissac estate agent who was to spend two days with us showing his collection. As dapper and impeccable as his car, he was dressed in a tan-coloured English corduroy suit the first time I'd met him last month, today it was black leather trousers worn with zippered trainers.

Then he'd zipped me round the country roads, preening and fiddling with his ear-lobe length grey-streaked hair, forever peering at himself in the mirror and tapping the steering wheel to Radio Nostalgie. In Moissac, Jean-Louis is cool.

Behind us in his office we had left his wife, a curvacious matron who gazed upon him with that curiously loving yet, exasperated gaze of a grown-up to her wayward infant. One knew instinctively though that if Jean-Louis started to act on his perceived image, her large hand would swot him as flat as any irritating fly.

He had no English and delighted in bumper hugging and blind corner overtaking. I put myself into a Zen state to cope; singing along with the radio as he beat the rhythm on the steering wheel and checked his errant locks.

We had seen several houses and I'd been deeply impressed with his flirtatious ways with the women of the house who obviously looked forward to his visits to pass the long, slow days. He did triple kisses (four and I think you take them home) but sadly I was not impressed with the houses.

In one house, down by the canal with the railway line just across from it, he and the young owner laughingly assured me that trains were few and far between. Unfortunately for them, three thundered past in the short time I was there. Jean-Louis shrugged - a gesture I was soon to become increasingly familiar with.

Finally we came to a farmhouse recently converted by a chief of police who had been re-assigned to the Reunion

Isle. A mixture of stone and Toulousian 'pink' brick dating back to the 17th century, it lay in a clutch of four houses on a lane, surrounded by fields growing artichokes. A few kilometres away was the busy village of St Nicolas de la Grave, with its imposing Mairie, a former castle owned by Richard the Lionheart.

Moissac was just ten minutes; Toulouse 40 minutes and Albi just over an hour. Its positioning could not have been more perfect although the land was much flatter than further on.

The wrought iron gate entrance was charming and the courtyard beyond, though overgrown, had once had a semblance of ordered planting imposed on it. But inside I saw the cracks, the awful shoddy workmanship, the pretence of a kitchen and the ominous stains around the radiators on the original terracotta tiles. I felt nothing for it and said my now almost reflexive 'non'.

But today I'm giving it a second chance, allowing Pierce to see the reality of what I've been looking at. Surprisingly Pierce is instantly taken with it and walking through the admittedly large rooms he lays out a vision of a potential four-bedroomed, three-bathroomed, galleried with library separate salon'd amazing house.

All I can sense is the smell of damp in at least three of the downstairs rooms and a dark, lingering presence in the oldest part of the house. Jean-Louis, snatching a last glance at himself in the bathroom mirror, is no fool. He works on my son. Up on the new mezzanine level where a door leads to an unconverted space with similar massive beams to the second 'cathedral,' brick-dressed sitting room, he lays out a vision of a suite for Pierce with bathroom and privacy.

When it comes to nudges, winks, girlfriends, pulling power, I now know men have a common language. Pierce has little French, Jean-Louis no English, but between them they are bonded in a testosterone-fuelled fantasy.

We return to the hotel where again, grovellingly grateful that my son likes the area, I listen to his plans and how easily the house could be turned into a beauty and I agree to return. A call to Jean-Louis organises a French builder to join us on site.

I admit that on third view I can see the potential, but this is a house already at the top end of my budget without pool or extras. The French builder has an even more localised accent than Jean-Louis. 'You don't even know your own name any more, do you?' says Pierce accusingly, as I stand sweating in the 'unfinished' space after half an hour explaining what has to be done. 'I thought you could speak French. You've lost it, haven't you?'

'Yes I have,' I stutter, sideways smiling at the stubby builder. 'I can't understand a bloody word he's saying. I don't really want this house and I can't build my life on you bringing girls 'home' for the week-end.'

Pierce and Jean-Louis shrug – the builder shrugs – and I can feel in their shared looks, their male contempt for my indecision. For a minute I allow them their sad macho bloody union. And then, drawing myself up to my full 5ft and a bit height, I said (in perfect classical French, sort of): 'Gentlemen, I am interested. Not at this price. Not at the state the house is in. I would like an estimate for the work to come and I would like it before I leave, in three to four days' time.

'I am not a fool. I do not have money to burn. This is not

my perfect house, but I am willing to see what can be done. And I want you to e-mail me a very specific estimate and I will consider it. Okay?'

Jean-Louis tosses a grey lock, the builder licks his pencil, Pierce casts his eyes up to heaven. I leave without a backward glance ready to get into the Mercedes. Jean-Louis turns up the jazz on the way back and winks at Pierce in the mirror with a look that says 'she'll do it.'

Oh, but I won't unless it is truly feasible. Is it unreasonable to want the coup de coeur, the heart-thumping knowledge that this is the one? If I get a good estimate from the builder, then it's possible. I am tired and I want a house and everybody tells me I have to compromise - so be it. But I don't feel excited and I just feel the need to get on with it. Again I wonder why I am so prepared to let my son pull my strings.

Almost 48 hours on, there is no word from the French builder and we're leaving the day after tomorrow. I have made a decision. No, it is nowhere near the perfect house, but given the right amount to make it so, I will buy it. The owner has agreed to drop €40,000, but no more and it now depends on the estimate.

I've taken pictures to show friends, but my heart is still not involved. I tell myself that it could be fantastic and yet, I feel nothing. I do feel annoyance with myself for failing to buy in France after all these weeks and months. I'm also worried that The Herald will pull the column if I don't pull my finger out.

Pierce is still waxing lyrically about his 'suite' and how he'll invite his girlfriends to 'his' place in France. Excuse me. He wants to pull in London with the line: 'Yes, my mother has a house in the South of France. You must come for the weekend. I have my own private suite.'

This is not enough for me to buy a house that doesn't inspire me. Over our last but one dinner before returning to the UK, I make this point. He looks at me with big eyes and says, as if speaking to someone mentally challenged: 'Mum, you have to commit. You've got a serious commitment problem. You have to stop this mad dash from one end of France to the other. You know you're going off your head. You've got to stop. Now.'

When did this pyscho-babble become part of normal speech? I am not off my head. I may be slightly manic, even rather deranged, but that's perfectly permissible in my present state of flux. I am determined to buy, but not at any cost. And as for commitment – I've had 25 long hard years of it.

We glare at each other across the table. 'I don't like the garden and I don't like the salon - it's creepy. I don't like... it,' I tell him in an increasingly childish whine. But, I'm worn down and I concede how it could be good, even great.

'Well there you go now – you're nearly there,' he says triumphantly. 'Let's do it. It could be fantastic. I'll come out when you move and help do things – you know, like painting and stuff. (The pigs of France would be flying high the day that happened.)

Maybe it could work. I join him in drawing plans on the napkins and I get slightly excited (again the large red is a help) and we head for bed with an amazing plan for the brick house.

Actually more a ludicrous extravagant 'grand designs'

plan involving 'his' glass bathroom; toughened glass balustrades to the mezzanine and an Aga I'll never use. The next morning I wake up with a sick feeling, not the pleasurable thrill of having found the right place. We are in a wonderful room overlooking the weir in Albi – the Cathedral dominating the window space. The sound of the water is both soothing and powerful.

'You're not smoking already are you?' grunts the heir from his twin bed. 'For God's sake.'

'No I'm not,' I say crossly exhaling through the open window. 'But if I were, so what? This is a smoking room. You smoke. I smoke and I'm paying. Anyway get up, I want to see this agent in Albi. This isn't a holiday you know.'

'Can you stop talking?' he groans. 'I've barely slept – you were snoring half the night and sleep-laughing the rest of it. I've had enough. I'm sick of France. I don't want bread for breakfast. I want food, real food and another four hours sleep.'

I should know better by now. But like a toreador piercing an already angry young bull, I goad: 'Bloody great. Is this what it's going to be like if I buy that house? Trying to get you to paint? You've been on the road barely a week, you've moaned non-stop and cost me a fortune. Well I've had enough, too. Be up, dressed and downstairs in half an hour or I'm off.'

And by now warming to my theme, I throw in: 'And another thing. I've changed my mind. I'm buying a one-bedroomed flat with a balcony. Just enough room for Portia. No room for you, no room for your friends. And when I die it'll go to the Cat and Dog Home.'

The sheets are now stuffed in his ears. 'Fine. Whatever,' he says.

I fling a last: 'I bloody mean it,' before slamming the door shut. Two-and-a-half hours later, on my third coffee nursing my wrath to keep it warm, I barely glance up as the lift doors open and he thuds into the seat next to me. Act 2.

'I feel sick,' he says. 'I need food.'

'Breakfast is finished,' I reply curtly. 'It's lunchtime.'

We sit in silence for another ten minutes. I crack first. 'Right, come on. There's a great restaurant opposite the Cathedral. You can get an omelette or something.' And on we go.

Two hours later, the sunshine, the omelette and the flirty, good-looking waitress have worked their magic for Pierce. The two reds have done the same for me. We're drawing plans again, using paper napkins from adjoining tables. Pierce's bathroom has now become a wet-room. The roll-top bath will be in the bedroom itself against a glass window overlooking the artichokes. My study will abut the mezzanine, glass desk keeping the theme going. Lavish bookcasing will line the gallery and the salon/library while paintings will be dramatically placed on the vast stone wall.

We really do deserve each other.

Chapter 6

IT takes two more weeks and several fretful, semi-incomprehensible phone calls to Jean-Louis before the French builder's estimate arrives. He may not have inspired much confidence with his tattered notebook, pencil and measure, but his devis, perfectly arranged on an e-mailed spread sheet does. Even in French, with numerous codicils and additions for tax and VAT, it is instantly apparent that his initial 'not much money, barely a month's work,' didn't make it to the first page.

Even with the very favourable £/€ rate at the time, it is roughly £50,000 and as far as I can make out that doesn't include our glass fantasies, new kitchen, or anything above plastic baths. Looking back I don't think he quite grasped the concept of wet-rooms and who can blame him? Most rural French houses have several unwanted ones.

I, of course, haven't the slightest idea of whether it is good, bad or indifferent. I can barely add up – I needed a calculator to do my expenses for heaven's sake. But I do know that I can't afford it and also running through my mind, fairly or unfairly, is that the French think we're all loaded, pretty stupid and willing to pay way over the odds.

So, now set on a course, I decide to send in a Brit builder, immediately going against all my pre-France notions of only using locals and avoiding the Anglos. Of course, I don't know any, but I call up the English owner of a rather splendid maison de maître, which was pointed out to me by Jean-Louis as we passed through a village close to where the brick house was.

'He and his wife run it as a châmbre d'hotes and the work they've done on it is superb,' he'd told me.

Back in my Wiltshire cottage with time running out I phone, explain what I'm doing and ask if they can recommend anyone to basically do a survey. It seems they have had a rocky ride with various builders over the years but they now have a man whose work is excellent. They give me his mobile and he agrees to contact Jean-Louis, but I still have to wait another three days before he can do anything. He too works on French time.

I'm naively confident he will be cheaper. I don't go into the glass fantasies at this stage, just ask him to view it structurally and give an overall price for the potential interior work as well. Of course, I don't ask his background, his qualifications, his previous works that I could maybe view on-line. That would seem so rude, wouldn't it?

Now that it is seeming to be slipping from my grasp I've almost become enthusiastic about the house, but that says more for my perverse nature than for any real desire. I cannot wait for his assessment and wing out pictures with what is to come to all and sundry.

When he phones, the Brit builder, Steve asks if I want him to be blunt. Absolutely. He's as blunt as a builder's bum. To sum it up, the pink bricked already 'renovated' house is a DIY mess and needs at least double the French builder's estimate to make it anywhere close to the dream pulling palace envisaged by my son.

All the renovated work will have to be ripped out and whole chunks of the exterior re-pointed. There is a major damp problem, the septic tank is ancient and tiny, the new plumbing and electrics are dangerously suspect and the pretty tiled roof is a total disaster.

'Basically,' says Steve, 'You'll have to treat it as a canvas and start all over again before you even touch the cosmetic stuff.' He drones on and on using builder terms which I encourage with a confident 'I see, I see,' as if I'm not a renovation virgin but a hardened old pro.

Now, given that the owner has said he will not go below £180,000, there isn't a cat in hell's chance that I can afford or be remotely interested in such a prospect. Hell again, I don't even want a renovation prospect. Suddenly there is a great part of me hugely relieved that I can walk away.

I phone Jean-Louis and we have our usual painful conversation. Between his fast bedongs and bedangs and my attempt at French building terms which involve sentences which would translate as: 'I mean the grey stuff which is placed between the bricks to keep them all happy and also to hold tight the outside without penetration...' it is a very, very long ten minutes.

But he obviously gets what I am saying, even though he doesn't agree with Steve's assessment of a property, which he is proudly selling as fully-renovated. Not just fully-renovated, but beautifully renovated by its proud owner. Fifteen minutes later he phones me back and basically says the owner will now sell for £140,000. Amazingly, he understands immediately my French equivalent of that much loved Glasgow phrase - 'On yer bike.'

However, we cannot let this house come between our blossoming friendship which I fear has many weeks yet to run, so I kindly tell Jean-Louis that like Napoleon I will return and try again. I swear I hear his heart drop at the prospect, but he hides it well with a nervous cough and the promise to boldly go and search for my heart's desire, not stopping until he drops in the attempt. Only French estate agents could make a house search sound like a crusade where the white knight girds his loins and mounts his trusty Merc clasping his lady's colours. I do hope Madame Jean-Louis is listening and appreciates this man.

I go back to the internet with the cold eye I now cast from experience on the agents' sites, and instead of salivating at stone cottages I find my lips curling in cynical despair. And then my new best builder friend, Steve, phones. I tell him I am not going forward with the house and of my conversation with Jean-Louis. He makes soothing noises between now calling me 'love,' 'darlin'' and 'sweetheart' in between sentences, which end with 'know what I mean?' I place his accent between Essex and Worcestershire and hide my irritation at his familiarity.

I'm always suspicious when people tell you how all the others will rip you off, pretend to get you a good deal, but that you're that rare animal, a straightforward, tell it like it is, professional. Suspicious because it's a line I've used often myself, God forgive me, in trying to get a story and get rid of the opposition. Never con a conner.

What he is suggesting is that I come over again very soon; he will introduce me to 'good' estate agents who don't rip off the Anglos - and - incidentally have I ever considered new build? For £165,000 I could have a four-bedroomed house, all high spec, two bathrooms and all done in traditional style, but with 'English' finishing and a ten-year guarantee.

I say I'm looking for character and history; have no desire to live in a cul-de-sac of new suburban houses surrounded by couples with 2.5 children whose highspot of the week-end is pressure-hosing the Peugeot. I do agree that great bathrooms and kitchen – a bizarre concept in rural France – are necessary points of happiness.

'Nah, nah,' he cuts in. 'We're not talkin' cul de sacs. You can get all you want darlin', trust me,' he says. 'I just happen to have a good contact with a building company you'd love. No skin off my nose. Know what I mean?'

Yes I do, darlin'. Now here's the rub. Were this happening in the UK, I'd ask him to send a bill in for looking at the house, thank him for his work, say no thanks and never deal with the man again. But, I'm open to all possibilities at this stage and despite the fact that he obviously thinks I'm a (as they say in France) pigeon for the plucking, I agree to phone him with arrival dates and take a tour.

After all he comes highly recommended. He apparently has connections with estate agents, French builders and local tradesmen. Maybe I have stumbled across a rare gem despite his patronising patter, of which he probably isn't even aware. Maybe he speaks the same way to men – dropping the 'darlin'', 'sweetheart' and 'love' for something like 'mate', or 'man'. Maybe I'm being far too cynical and this man feels compelled to help a poor single woman find that dream house where she and her dog can live in a golden glow of contentment and light candles to his goodness every Sunday in church. Yeah, right, mate.

However, the kennels have had a cancellation, I get another cheap flight, re-wash the handful of clothes I have here and prepare to set off yet again. Steve says not to organise any viewings of houses, he'll fix all that. Had I sounded a bit younger I'm sure he would have added the rider: 'Don't you worry your pretty little head about all that. You just leave it up to your Uncle Steve.'

'Let's face it darlin', a lot see you comin' and ratchet up that price,' he purrs on. 'I know the straight ones. You leave it all to me sweetheart. Phone me the second you get here. We'll have a glass of wine, a chat and tell you what, sweetheart, you'll go back with a house.' What a kind man.

I phone the son and tell him his pulling palace is a no-go. That I'm about to go back out again, but there's nothing that will persuade me to think about it. He is not happy and says again that irritating 'whatever' and I know that once back in London he has actually mentally dropped it into his mental pending file, dismissing it from his head as his own life takes over again. Which is how it should be.

Anyway he's about to go out he informs me as I quickly point out that for once I've been sensible and we, correction, I, could have been landed with a turkey if I hadn't got in the builders. 'No mum,' he says with the laboured sigh of a son cursed with such a mother. 'You're just in denial, aren't you? You never really wanted it anyway. So, got to go. Love you.'

And that's it. As usual after all the passion, the demands, the future according to Pierce, when I call a halt, it is done, dusted in an instant. Move on. I'm still pondering what that says about him, me, boys, mothers, as I drop off Portia, drive to Bristol, catch the now almost boring flight to Toulouse and end up back in my preferred catchment of Moissac. This time I'm staying in the chambre d'hôtes who recommended Steve.

It has been simply, but rather cleverly done. The mixture of plain Ikea bedroom furniture, glimpsed large sofas in downstairs family rooms with the odd decent piece of old furniture works well with the exquisite flooring both wood and tiles which grounds this old house. The owners have that look of strained exhaustion and detachment I've found in similar places around France. A combination of slight defiant low-level anger that they need to do this to survive mingled with a tired pride in what they've achieved.

As always, unless one finds instant open kindred spirits, it is an uneasy mix and tricky for guests to achieve the right level of paying clients and socially similar acquaintances. It is best to let the owners lead. This couple are too involved with their children and their lives to have any interest in me, so I sit quietly in my bedroom and wonder where I'll eat tonight.

The wife has already told me rather dismissively that nothing is open locally as she disappears to tend to her children, pointing the way to the breakfast room, which is included in the price. I've already played my Steve card as to why I'm here, thanks to them, but she just looks at me as if recalling a dim, distant memory.

It is a good job I have no desire to open such a place. I have no interest or ability in cooking, but I could never leave a person alone in a bedroom knowing there is nothing open locally. I would have to ask them to join 'us' for a meal and ultimately think nothing of doing so. But that's me and obviously not these people. So, wearily I head off to the village and buy some ham, a baguette and a couple of bottles of wine. I intend to have a glass or three on the terrace which is featured in their website and have some in reserve to offer one or three to anyone who joins me there.

Even now I cringe at the memory. It is clear, despite what the website says that they consider this their private property, not the 'welcoming guest terrace' to sit and view the sunset. They are preparing a barbeque and the children are flinging themselves into an above-ground pool, staring unkindly at this poor woman who has insinuated herself onto a chair in the corner of their life.

I stare at the sky as no one greets me and yet again I wonder what the hell I am doing here. I slink back to my room and return after a decent time when they will have finished eating. This time the host joins me and accepts a glass from my bottle.

We discuss Steve and it is obvious that all has not gone well with the work he has done for them. I decide cruelly that it's time to say I'm a journalist and watch the change in attitude. It is electric. Suddenly I'm of interest and the host disappears to find a decent bottle of his own, obviously chivvying up his wife to return now that I may be of value.

He talks of his plans to use the house for bridge and cookery weekends, suggesting I could write pieces for the British nationals. I pretend to ponder and agree while thinking not a chance mate, even if I could flog the story on. If in the downtimes you cannot greet and genuinely make welcome the lone, stray woman, then why should you be given national space as if you were a haven of warmth?

As we sip and I learn more about them and why they are here, I do feel a better understanding of their plight. They, like many ex-pats, believed they could live a country life in a French manor house after their Surrey semi and then, when money ran out, had to think of other means to sustain it. But I cannot forgive their chilly and off-handed welcome to a paying client who is helping them sustain their life. Just as I find rather distasteful their sudden bonhomie in discovering I am a journalist; someone who could be of some use.

The next morning I sit on the main steps in light sunshine awaiting Steve. The house behind me is empty. The children in school, the husband and wife off and about whatever they do here and an old French woman the only sign of life as she clears up my meagre breakfast tray.

My backside grows numb and Steve's mobile just goes to message service. I thought I was meeting a representative of the new-build builder. I thought Steve was coming with her. Eventually I get Steve, he gets her and there is a garbled conversation about dates being misunderstood. He will be here tomorrow, and once more after yet another miserable night I am sitting waiting on the stone steps.

'Sorry pet,' he breathes on the mobile when he finally answers on the fifth call. 'I'm up to my bloody eyes, but I'll make it up to you tonight. What if I take you out to dinner, eh darlin'? Whatever you want. 'We'll talk then. Honest sweetheart, I'll find you the home of yer dreams. Okay, pet?'

No, I tell him, I'll meet you tomorrow outside the

chambre d'hôtes. So I wait on the same steps the following day. The subsequent conversation is a virtual re-run of the day before and the day before that. This time he is promising me champagne when we meet.

I give it one last day and sit silently on the steps again. Yet another hour after the appointed time I ring his mobile and hear more excuses about being stuck on a job, but close to a finish and he's on his way. We'll have a fine meal on him. My backside is as cold as my answer.

'No pet,' I mimic. 'If you can't turn up for an initial meeting, then I'd never trust you to build me something on time. I don't need taking out to dinner, don't need champagne and, you know what darlin', I don't need you actually.'

I'm as stunned at my statement as he obviously is, but I click off on my mobile before he can respond. I'm shaking because for all my apparent chutzpah, I'm really a pathetic soul who hates confrontation. But I've done it and it gives me great pleasure to tell my host and hostess that their recommended man is an arse. The man flushes and agrees he's discovered that himself and he's so, so sorry.

This, of course, will not affect anything I may write about them, will it, he asks anxiously. Of course not, I lie, just wanting to spend my last night on their far too, too thin bloody Ikea mattress.

By lunchtime the following day I'm back in Le Moulin at Moissac where the welcome is as warm as the last one was cold. Bless him. Jean-Louis recovers quickly from his initial look of horror as he sees me crossing the road to his office. 'Madame Cook! ça va?', hand outstretched for the obligatory formal handshake. Madame Jean-Louis grins wickedly from behind the counter, happy, as usual, I fantasise, with his discomfort.

We don't discuss the fiasco of the pink brick house. He just pilots me towards the Merc - despite no appointment - with a last look of dismay, or maybe silent cry for help, at his grinning wife. Today, although it is around 70 degrees, he is wearing a beautifully cut pin-stripe suit, a blue cotton weave shirt and shiny, shiny black brogues which I'm sure are Church's.

So, Jean-Louis and I make our now-familiar tortured, banal conversation and then thankfully he switches on a blues CD and we merrily sing along instead. Neither of us can actually sing, but it beats trying to communicate. Midway through a chorus of 'There is a House in New Orleans,' I cannot believe we are passing close enough to see the two vast nuclear power chimneys with their belching steam on our way to see what he enthusiastically describes as a 'magnificent medieval house with pigonnier', which I will love.

He shrugs at my shocked face, pointed finger and non, non, non. And then we turn into a sort of overgrown garden with a gigantic brick building with columbage (think exterior Tudor timber beams) attached to a bulging three story pigonnier which has steel belts around it to keep it upright.

As usual he stands and using his arms like a windmill points out north, south, east, west. He doesn't need to point out the chimneys as they're still in my face. Then we're inside. There are five, dark large rooms with fireplaces. One has been newly fitted as a kitchen – think 70s brown wood, 'country-style' MFI, the height of chic hereabouts. There are also bowls of pellets placed in every room – think rats, hopefully just mice.

The piece de resistance is apparently up a rickety stair. Voila – we are in the grenier, the attic, an enormous room with worm and termite-ridden massive beams and at least one hundred generations of spiders judging by the cobwebs which are so ornate they could have been sprayed there as the backdrop to a horror film.

Jean-Louis rocks back on his shiny heels, extends his arms in a victory flourish and says: 'Magnifique... non?' I feel we know each other well enough by now to ask him if he has gone mad, or does he think I have?

He looks hurt, and the weight of his crusading task to find me a place hangs heavy on his deflated shoulders. I look at his beautiful shoes, dusty now in his climb up the stairs. I feel a really bad person, but indicate by a sharp twitch of the head that it's time to go.

I have a fag and a cough as he brushes from his suit the ancient dust before telling me I should give up. What? House searching? No. Fags.

I'll draw a veil over what was to come except to say that he takes me to see a series of totally unsuitable houses expressing further shocked hurt each time I say 'non'.

And finally, as if tiring of the game, he drives me to the hills above Moissac and stops outside somewhere hidden beyond a magnificent stretch of 14ft hedge, private car gate and separate entrance.

The owner is called by mobile from her shopping trip and we walk into a hidden garden – actually a wonderful two, three acre paradise bounded by wood, orchard, shady nooks and crannies. Away from the house to the back is a huge open barn, which would make a house in itself.

Perfectly positioned amidst this splendour is an almost Provençal long house with both open and covered verandahs typical of the region, but now rare to find.

Hens cluck in a far corner, their busy voices mingling with the hypnotic buzz of bees, and Jean-Louis, ignoring his beautiful shoes, walks the territory pointing out through the woods where mushrooms can be gathered. It is the first time I feel I've found what I'm looking for. But it is cruel, because it is £70,000 over what I can afford at my maximum. A maximum, which leaves me with nothing - not a centime.

I utter a silent prayer as we wait for the owner sitting on the verandah enjoying the warmth of the sun and the sound of the birds. Please, please God, let the house be perfect needing nothing but me, Portia and the books and I'll work it out somehow. I could even live with the large, unsightly over-ground pool and already I'm planning a party based in the open barn, which has already seen many I would guess judging by the string of fairy lights strung across its length.

At last she arrives and we enter through a kitchen, which has seen better days. I feel a pang of disappointment almost immediately. It is as if two different hands, two different minds have created house and grounds.

There is a surprising ugliness in both the furnishings and the proportions of the rooms. The woman is perhaps in her 40s and has teenage children, but the feel of the place is that of an old person's. There is a bedroom off the sitting room and another door takes us into a hall and corridor leading to a cramped bathroom with a cheap shower compartment where the tiles are chipped and the grout ingrained with usage. It is the only bathroom in the house.

Downstairs and along another corridor we come to a bizarre second kitchen dining room with glass doors on to the garden. Jean-Louis says it would not take much to fully fit the kitchen and the one in the main part could be turned back into a hall. Upstairs there are two cramped bedrooms and a third half-completed out of the attic. It has a beautiful new wooden floor and windows which overlook the length of the grounds. He opens another door into more attic space and shows how easily another bathroom could be put in here.

I walk around again. The books could be housed in the strange dining-room, the bathroom would have to be blitzed and it is plain, because of the smell, that yet again there is a damp problem seeping away under the twisty corridors. The house could be liveable instantly, but not happily and not terribly comfortably. However, it might be worth it just for this hidden garden and for being so close to Moissac.

It has also been on the market only six days, so no chance to deal and negotiate a price, which would have to be almost insultingly below the demand price. It is also a house the French will buy quickly and not one that will hang around. As Jean-Louis and I take another stroll around the garden away from the owner, I put all these thoughts to him.

Unfortunately he agrees. I look at him in mute accusation. As always, he shrugs. I realise, despite everything I've told him, he thinks I'm a player and have a lot more cash than I have. He has bought into the belief that all us Brits have a long stocking when it comes to buying houses.

When I mention that the upkeep of the grounds would be a fortune in itself, he tells me that if I buy it he will come with his own sit-on lawn mower and take care of the garden himself. Of course I laugh and wonder which designer Jean-Louis would pick for his gardening outfit.

But I walk away, sick, unhappy and unable to find the clever words I have in English to translate into French to get this house for a price that would work. We drive back to Moissac in silence without even a chorus of the House of the Rising Sun to break our contemplation.

We stand on the pavement outside his office, me looking in his windows in case there's something he's keeping from me as he did the last one. But everything that catches my eye is double or more the price I can afford. The whole point of coming here is to be mortgage free and anyway who would give me a mortgage now that I don't have the might of Associated Newspapers' pay cheque behind me. Even if I could raise a comparatively small mortgage I have no idea what I'll earn, if I'll earn, in this backwater.

All my newspaper contacts swear they'll use me and back it up with tales of how often they need people to move quickly in that part of France and how hard it has been in the past. But unless one were to give me a retainer, I cannot base anything on words alone.

That night as I sit over my solitary meal in Le Moulin I think how right Helene, the estate agent from Montauban had been in her summing up me and my situation when I'd contacted her in the first months of my search.

We'd met in my hotel just off the main square in Mountauban. She was probably early 60s, with clipped grey hair, blazer, jeans, white shirt with spotted cravat. By the end of the day I was to learn that she used all her names – Hildegarde, Marie Louise, Helen or Helene –

depending on which clients she was seeing - German, French, English or Irish. She was a very clever estate agent and I liked her.

Within ten minutes over coffee she understood exactly what I was looking for, shuffled to one side the major part of the houses she'd initially picked for me and told me bluntly that I had champagne tastes and beer money. And had I ever considered North Africa?

In her car on our tour of the area in which I now knew I wanted to live, she talked about everything from the upcoming French Presidential elections, the war in Iraq, Christian/Muslim plain chant of the 17th century, the best tagines in Toulouse and the political correctness of modern day Britain and Tony Blair. Even better she matched me fag for fag, cough for cough.

I would love to imply that we had such an erudite conversation in French. No, her English was impeccable. A German, she'd lived in London with her first husband during the late 60s. Her children, now grown up, were scattered between Casablanca, Paris and Frankfurt. In maybe a year's time she was planning to leave her rented flat and move to Casablanca. She followed her feelings.

Amusing, laconic and once assured that our views on Bush and Blair were the same, she was a mine of the useless information I adore.

Pointing to a large abbey in the hills she told me she'd sold it a few years ago to an Englishman, a musician, who planned to convert it. Alone and no doubt overwhelmed by what he'd taken on he started to drink.

'It wasn't long before he was drinking from the moment he got up,' she said.' 'He called me back a few months ago.

The place was a wreck – beer bottles everywhere. He has done nothing.' She paused to muse on why he was killing himself on beer instead of the local wine before continuing: 'Now he wants €1.3 million for it – not a cent less.'

You know, she said, while there are plenty of foreigners who make a great success of life here, there are many tragedies being played out too. 'I loved my time in England. Who wouldn't in the 60s, but something has happened to the British. Once you were known for your good manners. Now...' she gave the shrug that needs no words.

'I think it is the drinking. The young ones are more obvious. I dread getting a table in a restaurant next to a group of Brits. Some seem to have only one aim - to get drunk. Why is that? Is life so bad there now?'

Sometimes you only realise how bad something has become when you see the absence of it. Night after night in the numerous restaurants I've visited on these trips I have been struck by the combination of muted conversation, gentle laughter, and the use of alcohol as a pleasure not a need. I have never seen anyone even slightly tipsy never mind drunk.

In a Chinese restaurant outside Agen, I watched a large group of 20-something-year-old men arrive late and take over a centre table. As far as I could see they had one bottle of beer each and several carafes of water. There was none of the shouting and swearing we've sadly come to expect in England or Scotland.

In other places I've noticed couples of all ages enjoying a cocktail before dinner and occasionally a half-bottle of wine. I have never seen tables groaning with the bottles that seem compulsory on our nights out.

Fastidiously private, the French find raised voices in restaurants a gross discourtesy; children are instantly reprimanded for cutting across their parents' conversation and must remain at the table until all are finished. Waiters are treated with respect, their views on the food sought and they return this respect with pride in their performance. It is not in the expectation either of a good tip. Tipping is not really done - only a few coins if really happy with the meal.

Even in one of the trendiest café/bars in Toulouse, where students pour in after 5pm, I noticed more espressos and waters than beer or spirits. Sure, like all students, they chatter as much on their mobiles as to their friends, but the level is kept low and eyes constantly check that their talk is not upsetting nearby tables.

And there isn't that undercurrent of repressed anger that ripples through our pubs as the night wears on and the drink increases.

I discussed all this with Helene. She nodded agreement and asked again: 'So what is happening in Britain? Is life so bad there now?'

For once I didn't have an answer. The truth is that it is only by coming here I see how often abnormal our normal has become.

Draining my own glass I feel a slight unease at how much my own consumption of wine has increased on these trips. That, and the rich food I'm eating in hotel restaurants are showing in a definite weight increase. And that is definitely worrying. Tomorrow it's back on the plane and back on the internet. This is starting to become a chore.

Chapter 7

IT is two more long weeks before I can face returning to France. I'm getting embarrassed at fielding the calls from friends who can't understand what's holding me back. All this faffing around is so unlike me is their underlying implication, and I know that too. Every house or flat I've ever bought has been known with a snap of the fingers and the absolute certain knowledge that it is the one.

But nothing is doing it there for me and I'm also haemorrhaging cash with this constant to-ing and fro-ing. I pick up the phone and call an estate agent in a place called Lavit de Lomagne - a biggish village about 20 minutes from Moissac and say I'll be there on Thursday.

It isn't love at first sight. There's no gut-churning, dizzy, out-of-control lust that makes me want Las Molières no matter what. It sort of looms out of the countryside - a big chunk of buff-painted stone farmhouse, closely protected by five ancient chestnut trees.

But it is the first house that does not have to be reached

by a tortuous drive, or one that is hemmed in by threatening bushes and overgrown gardens. It is open and clean. To get to it we've come from Lavit, dipped in to a prosperous valley and climbed to a hamlet where a small church, almost Mexican in its simplicity, stands guardian.

We skirt it, climbing upwards and down again and up until, rounding a curve, we reach a crossroads dominated by one of the large crosses which appear everywhere without, as far as I can see, any obvious religious significance.

Straight ahead, sitting in fields not lawns, is the house. A chain across the drive is the only impediment to its unfenced four-acre site and I recognise cypress trees, mimosa, palm trees, even an olive tree planted haphazardly in the French way.

Hedges and deep fosses (ditches) provide a natural perimeter to the land which, to the South West stretches to a boundary shared with a pretty Hansel and Gretel style cottage; a verandah created by its low overhanging roof held up by sturdy beams. It too is shuttered and barred and the estate agent tells me it's a holiday home owned by a young English couple.

Looking for miles in a 360-degree sweep, I can see the outlines of farms and the top of a roof. Hills, mere hillocks from here, rise from other valleys flattened out from this high spot. The sky is vast and jet plumes criss-cross the blue, leaving and landing at Toulouse's airport an hour away.

Getting out of the car I notice irises against one wall and lizards streak away from my footsteps. Like many shuttered French houses, it hides itself in an unblinking, bland facade, having none of the coy, vine-clad flirtatiousness of many houses I've seen - and rejected - on entering their dank, dark interiors.

There seem to be no sweet little corners topped by ancient tiled overhangs here. No remnants of barns, pigeonniers, wells, or planted arbours and long lost vegetable gardens. No old bricks or exquisite individual stone facings. In fact, not one desirable attribute.

It has a peculiar rawness, despite the lush fields of wheat and soon to be sunflowers around it. The original house has the pretty Roman tiles of the region, but the newer two-storey addition does not. There is an ominous darker patch of buff ending in a sort of tide line all around the house, but estate agent, Jezza assures me it is 'splashback' from the 'pas normale' recent rainstorms.

It is everything I know I don't want – everything I said I would not even be looking at when I drew up my mental list. I know that come the night, the sky will be a silent, an even more vast, velvet cloak which will smother me in fear and supernatural terror.

The pretty cypresses lining one side of the potted tarmac drive will become fingers of dark foreboding, eerie sentinels signalling a path to nothingness. The chestnuts will curl in towards me in the dark, no longer guardians, but more prison wardens overlooking my cell.

The grounds - or rather fields with their mole-ridden clay piles - demand attention and constant cosseting. Constant mowing at least. They need more than pre-planted large terracotta pots bought from a garden centre. They need a woman who can dig and plant hour after hour; one who knows a weed from a flower. Or rather a landscape gardener and his workers who will dig, plant and nurture, hour after hour.

For I am not that woman. In the fantasy created by myself and now by The Herald readers who e-mail me urging me on, I am that woman. But I'm not. I should be because it apparently fits the next stage in baby boomer woman's life and so far I've fulfilled all the requirements. Except the one that says I should now be getting in touch with my true womanly self and wanting to plunge my hands into the earth, wanting to grow vegetables and fruit as an expression of my previously denied fecundity. Balls. Some things will never change.

Knowing all this, why can't I just walk away or refuse to get out of the car as I have done on several occasions? Las Molières is casting a spell, inviting me in. Like the ugly, yet somehow compelling guy who seduced you with a depth of promise far beyond the pretty boys, it makes me think twice; makes me look back over my shoulder as I try to walk away; gives a big enough twitch to my heart, if not my brain, to return – curious, uncertain, destabilised.

Jezza and her daughter, Vanessa are meanwhile trying to penetrate numerous grills and locks with a fistful of keys to get us inside. There is a lot of sighing, eye-rolling and French too rapid for me to follow. I find myself edgily anxious to enter this difficult, fawn-shuttered square of a house with a tacked-on wing and a tacked-on garage, joined under an iron and faux-tiled roof at the back to create a large courtyard.

The asking price is a massive £80,000 over my maximum and I'd picked it out after a day of bad choices. The agent didn't offer it to me. I saw it on her board, quite liked the obviously large, if over-wood panelled interior, and the over-enthusiastic description. And knowing that one should go in at least 20 per cent under on a price, I thought, why not?

Jezza paused when I pointed it out, thought about it,and said it could be possible. The owner, an Englishman, was fairly desperate to sell after only six months on the market. He had bought the house two years ago as a holiday home following renovations by a French couple who had lived in it for almost ten years. He, and his family, had now relocated to Jakarta and it was no longer feasible as a weekend getaway from London.

While Vanessa, continues trying to unlock the house, we walk around to the garage. Inside is an almost brand-new sit-on lawnmower and some boys' toys – like mountain bikes, basketball nets, table-tennis equipment and even a Gemini boat. Outside is a large, ugly, startlingly blue, overground pool surrounded by cheap decking with the backdrop of unrendered house and garage.

Beyond it and to one side, at last, something quirky and old. I'm not sure quite what it is. A three-doored pig pen under rose tiles and columbage? A goose pen? A stable for miniature horses? It's quaint even though one 'loose box' is the home of a reassuringly large oil tank for the central heating.

I walk back and stand looking at the two 'wings' of the house, the interior courtyard and the pitched faux-tiled roof linking both. In my imaginary world of possibilities, I can see a full-length glass wall, a gallery, a drawing room, electric shutters to close with the sun. It would be a load of cash expended on a fairly unattractive nothing really. A load of cash I do not have. Silk purse and sow's ear come to mind.

Meanwhile Vanessa fails to open the locks. I do idly wonder why there are so many, but rationalise it's a holiday home and insurance has to be involved. We agree to return tomorrow, when a friend of the owner, a British builder, will open all doors. I feel somehow cheated, but prepared to return as I stroll away, looking back over my shoulder and wondering why I am drawn to this big brute, which has nothing I have fantasised about.

An ominous heavy buzzing comes from the first of the chestnut trees – the one closest to the drive and the house. Do wasps nest in trees? A sudden warm breeze ripples the fields and I feel again the peculiar stirring that this is meant to be. Still I don't feel love or even excitement – just the knowledge that I want to come back and see its interior.

A time is arranged and I return to Moissac and Le Moulin with a very, very slight churning in the stomach, wondering if this could be the house. Apart from La Maison de Merles, it's the only one so far I want to see again. And I know it's probably for all the wrong reasons. I had been writing this 'follow the dream' column for several months now and it's getting embarrassing because it's very obvious I'm going nowhere.

The readers must be getting bored. I'm getting bloody bored. I'm also getting worried. If I don't start living the bloody dream soon The Herald may pull the column and I'll really have a financial problem. Often I think if I didn't have the column, would I just quietly sneak 'home' again? Now, there's a thought. Sneak home to where though? Suffer the shame of the abrupt ending of a column with the words - sorry, changed my mind?

Later in the day I decide to go back alone in my hire car, stepping over the chain. There is no crack in any shutter that allows me even a glimpse of the interior. The sun is hot although it's only April and there's that strange heavy sense of watching and waiting that you feel when you are in isolated countryside. It seems there is a whole other world existing simultaneously. The only birds I'm aware of are birds of prey who perch for a moment on the electricity lines which also cross the land. Nobody passes the whole time I am there.

Again I tick off everything that is wrong with it and imagine myself sitting inside, quaking as a storm unleashes itself outside. To my astonishment I hear myself say, 'I could do that.'

Surprisingly reluctant to leave, I decide to drive along the nearby mysterious roads and meander around stunning wooded farmland with views that stretch into cultivated vales, dotted with tiny hamlets, topped by bastide villages shimmering in the heat haze.

At one point I look left, out over to countryside which stretches on and on and on as if the whole of France herself was opening out. Yet, everything around here seems deliberately hidden, unfolding itself only to those who've come off-road to idle away time.

I go back again to the house, parking at different spots on the two single-track roads which pass it. I count 20 trees in all, most unrecognisable to me, and once again draw up to walk around its indifferent bulk. My mind is now running on grand schemes. Terraces will have to be laid where tarmac and gravel sit ill at ease with the grass. Fencing of some kind for Portia; a proper pool excavated; hedging; more trees - the list is endless. And this is before I've even seen inside and for a price so far over my budget it is a joke.

So I leave. After all, it isn't love, is it? Perhaps I should just tell the agent I won't bother coming back tomorrow? Before the house goes out of sight through the rear mirror, I stop the car for yet another look back. Las Molières returns my stare, inscrutable.

By the time I get back to Le Moulin and my usual solitary meal in the half-empty dining room I have decided I may as well at least see inside. At least it would give me an idea as to what's on offer for €320,000.

The next morning when I call in at Cabinet International, Jezza's mother Gloria is waiting to take me back to Las Molières. It appears she has the equivalent of power of attorney granted to her by the owner. She started this business with her English husband in the late 60s and rightly sees herself as the doyenne of immobiliers in the Tarn et Garonne – probably in the whole of France.

It's another hot, glorious day as we drive out of Lavit and dipping in and out of the valleys patch-worked with rotational crops, we could be travelling through a 1950s picture postcard of unchanging rural life. Gloria chatters non-stop, extolling the virtues of the house as I listen uncritically more aware of the crimson flashes of wild poppies in the hedgerows; following the buzzards circling up high; squinting at the distant villages. Her driving leaves me clutching the armrest.

So it takes a few seconds before I realise that the welcoming, open-shuttered house on the hill is Las Molières. Gone is the indifferent bulk of yesterday. It's as if she has put on her best dress and make-up to entice and apologise for seeming rather standoffish and cool during my last visit. It is at last, the first time a house makes my stomach lurch.

A part of me had hoped that the good night's sleep and relentless internal monologue would have had me spurning her by dawn. Instead, I'm here, desperate to see what's inside, yet half-hoping it's so awful I'll run away again.

The English builder friend of the owner has made sure he got there before us, unlocking every window and door so that the sunshine warms and brightens the interior.

I step inside the now revealed half-paned glass front door, and breathe in. Nothing. It's the first house I have entered where there's no instant intake of that damp, mouldering smell of rot – the foul breath of a house that's had enough.

I'm in a wood-lined hall with two corridors leading off, and a fully-paned glass door which opens on to a terracotta kitchen and dining room running the width of the house. A miller's stair, almost ladder-like, leads upstairs. Glass double doors open to the front and in all there are three windows, two opening into the courtyard, one looking back at the stable.

It's the heart of the house, begging for my elm table and chairs. Two walls could be entirely covered with bookcases, another is just demanding pictures. The kitchen at the far end is behind a sort of half-wall into which is fitted two moulded basins under a single curved stainless-steel tap. The units under it and on one wall are few and could best be described as antique brown-country look, the kind last fashionable in the UK in the early 70s. An oven is built into the upright and there's a hob embedded in a counter top, which has space underneath for dishes and plates. Behind another door is a utility room with a massive and seemingly new central heating boiler.

But running the length of one wall from the end of the kitchen to the stairs, and projecting a good three feet, is a curious formica ledge on an apparently solid base. 'It's the old mangère,' says Gloria dismissively. 'Where the cows would have fed. This was the stable and the stairs led up to where the hay and straw would have been kept.'

Which was also presumably why the floor sloped quite alarmingly downhill. Easy sluicing out perhaps? 'It's a terrible waste of space though isn't it?' I suggest. 'I suppose they can be taken out?'

'Yes, yes,' said Gloria with a quick look at the builder who is starting to avoid my eyes. 'There are probably pipes and electrics running through them,' he mutters.

'Mmm,' I nod, studying and tapping the mangère. No one here was going to think I didn't know about all these things. I may be an ignorant fool in building matters, but they didn't know that. Oh yes, I know how to play hard-ball.

Off this room up a little step is the sitting room, disappointingly small, but with two windows to the front and the side and a simple fireplace with a wood-burning stove. Like the main room, heavy ancient oak beams criss-cross a ceiling, which goes full-height almost in an apex. An odd, though pleasant, black wrought iron balcony looks down from above and I can see another diamond paned door leading in to what presumably is the attic. More importantly I can visualise bookcasing extending along the East wall, over and above the window.

Underneath the balcony is another wooden, heavily-latched door which leads in to the main bedroom. Again 'French' doors lead out to the side and the tiles here are older, the original floor - well most of it - of what is probably a 200-year-old building. The house is still furnished and Gloria explains the price includes the furniture. There is nothing I would be interested in as I'm still wondering where all mine will go.

Off the bedroom through an un-doored doorway is the bathroom. I smell the chemical odour of a cheap room spray, but don't think too much about it. The room is adequate, with a tacky, though mercifully white, lavatory, corner bath and vanity unity cum basin with a string of Hollywood style lights above the mirror. A good-sized window floods more light in.

We go back to the hall, pushed out and on by Gloria. Down the corridor to the left is the main bathroom – again cheap fittings, but white. There is no shower and again a mangère topped with tiles instead of formica. Only a small almost ceiling-height window illuminates the quite large room.

At the end of the corridor the door opens on to what has obviously been the children's room. It's big, square and has a new, if cheap, wooden floor. I'm immediately struck by the continuation of the mangère. The whole annexe was obviously a much later added byre and the upright beam dividing the twin beds, plainly the remnant of stalls.

Like the bathroom two small high windows give on to the courtyard, but there are also two large windows looking to the front of the house and the back. This room has the impermanent look of a holiday house – a bedroom to crawl into and quickly fall asleep after a long day in the sun.

Back in the tiled hall the second small corridor leads to a back door into the courtyard, but before reaching it a door to the right opens to reveal a lavatory and little sink.

Now Gloria is leading me upstairs to the old hay store. The old trap door through which the fodder would have been pitched down, has been opened up and a wrought iron railing and upper banister gives a solidity it doesn't deserve. We're in the roof-space of the house, but a glass door on to a verandah stretching the full length of the annexe under the strutted, barn roof, brings much needed light. One end pitches down to around three feet, but there is ample room for a study and another full-height wall perfect for bookcases.

A step up takes you on to the bizarre wrought-iron balcony to peer down into the sitting room. The diamond-glassed door opens into a pristine attic, which I barely glance at, but figure could make another bedroom or bathroom. Stepping back down to what I am now thinking of as the study there is another glass-paned door, which opens into a large, beam crossed bedroom. The wall looking out on to the courtyard and the countryside beyond has an enormous window and fixed insect screen.

Cranking open the door on to the verandah, or really just a balustraded enormous space with a window opening East and a view as far as Lavit across the valleys, it's clear that this was where on wet days the children played table tennis. There's a discarded ball and bats, and suddenly I see the potential of a library cum drawing room, glass wall at the end, new proper stairs up from the hall or kitchen and ...so on.

I also see the possibility again of creating upon the template of this enormous roof an amazing extension involving glass again, stone, wood – drawing room, library, kitchen, atrium. Get a bloody grip. Je suis un rock star? Non.

However, as my brain often lives an entirely different life from the one me and my finances inhabit, it forces me to suggest such musings to the builder in a languid, though extraordinarily knowledgeable, way. 'One could, couldn't one?' I ask, patently implying in that lazy professional manner that I not only know the answer, the various techniques but also the cost right down to the last screw.

'Yeah. We had the same idea, that was plan B,' he says as we gaze at the iron struts holding up the roof. Pros both, we stare away and I ask: 'How much?' 'Minimum 50,000,' he says after a pause.

'Euros?'

'Sterling.' I do another couple of considered nods and wiggle my hand, adding a wry smile as if to challenge him a few thousand here or there.

'And suppose, just suppose,' I drawl. 'I just put a library or sitting room in a shell under the roof, where we're now standing?'

'It's 15,000... sterling.'

I nod again, but this time throw in the sideways glance and quizzical look, which can be taken whatever way he wants. It's a very clever tactic which suggests - don't mess with me boy. You and I both know exactly what it will cost.

Of course I haven't a clue. I can be shocked at the price of a loaf when someone tells me how much it costs, and blithely think £300 is a fair price for a pair of classic boots you'll wear for years.

I leave Gloria and the builder upstairs as I walk around

again - alone with a thoughtful, though sceptical, expression on my face in case they're watching me. I even pace out measurements and knock on walls or peer intently at the beams for long moments. God knows why, but I know that's what you do.

On the second circuit I'm increasingly aware that this house is a wood pervert's dream. There are planks, tongue and grooving, rough panels over every possible surface. Above the fireplace in the sitting room is a half-wall of pine tongue and grooving. Another wooden 'arm' stretches out from it with a bare light bulb dangling off the end on a wire. There is just one plug in the room, but a bizarre 'kitchen' cupboard three quarters of the way up the southern wall opens to reveal a junction box. Peering through the window I see the wires lead direct to the hideous concrete pylon in between the chestnut trees.

Even I know that this must be the main electricity cable into the house. I can't really think about this now, so I go back to the big main room. It's a bit like Heidi's cabin. The three solid, uneven oak beams are great. But the new thin 'beams' running lengthways are narrow, hideous pine holding up the floor in the 'study.' So is it the wood of the ceiling, or the floor of the study? It's as raw as the day it was put in.

Gloria has come downstairs and after 40-odd years in the business of selling to Brits, reads my mind and says: 'Beautiful, beautiful wood. Not cheap. Nothing cheap here.' She looks me straight in the eye with the clear conscience of an estate agent.

Between the beams in the sitting room and the upper bedroom and 'study,' the 'wood' looks like compressed hardboard. 'Insulation,' says Gloria quickly. 'A Northern French thing - marvellous.'

'Er, ugly?'

'Non, non,' she replies, her voice rising as if talking to an imbecile. 'Very clever. Very good.'

Again I stand in the main room, picturing my books lining the wall. This house can take my books. The first that can. Right. The above-ground pool would be fine for this year, but as I've said from the start I want a real pool. Minimum £15,000. I always round down.

Am I actually looking at this house as if it's a possibility? It's on sale for roughly £225,000, including furniture. I can go to a maximum of £180,000; still £20,000 over what I had promised myself I wouldn't spend and that could still allow me just enough to do the library/verandah.

That would mean of course that I would not have a cent left to augment the two cashed-in early pensions or give me any cloth to cut in emergencies. I also have to add on the eight per cent notaire's fees, which includes our equivalent of Stamp Duty and so on.

One last walk around. They've been quite clever in simply painting everything white, but the wood in the rooms is pretty overpowering. There's the usual visible pipework but most could be covered by the bookcasing.

Outside I remind myself that I was looking for a stone or Toulousean brick house; a pretty house, not this. No it definitely isn't love, but...

Gloria and I get back into the car and drive to her office. By the time we get there I say I'm prepared to make an offer.

Suddenly Jezza is back in the frame – she is the one who

will negotiate, not Gloria, who disappears back to her office. I write the offer down in euros and shove it across the table. It is the equivalent of £170,000 – almost £60,000 under the asking price. I point out that I am not interested in the furniture and though I'm keen, I will walk away.

She nods. Good sign. She will need to fax the owner in Jakarta. It could take days. 'No problem,' I say, attempting a bored lilt to my voice. 'I'm going to see friends four hours drive away and look at some other houses. I'll take a week-end out.'

I see her register the 'other houses' remark as I intended, so we shake hands and I drive back once more to Moissac. The tall, kind receptionist who knew where I was going today looks at me and asks hopefully: 'Well?'

I say: 'Yes, yes, I think I've found it,' and grin rather inanely at her.

She shrieks and clasps my hand pulling me forward for the two-cheek kiss. The maître d' comes through the dining room door and quickly assesses the situation. She orders a glass of champagne for me in celebration. The waiters come out of the dining room to shake my hand, genuinely pleased for me. I tell them it's not certain, that it will depend on the price and it's not really what I saw myself buying, but realise I'm shaking. Realise I may actually have gone and done it.

I go to my bedroom and start to phone or text. 'I've put an offer in on a house.' Again I find myself saying: 'It's not pretty. It's not what I thought I'd go for, but it has something. Well, it has space for the books and I can put a proper pool in. And it has white baths. I do love the countryside. Yeah, a lot of land. I know, I know, but I think

I'll be fine. I can see other houses, just.'

At dinner I drink too much and tippy-toe to bed quietly, giggling to myself as I undress. 'I have a house in France,' I say, several times, testing the phrase sobering up fairly rapidly when I realise I actually could have one. Can I really face the reality?

In bed, I can't sleep and re-read the guide book for the area. I go over every room in the house and find them all lacking. I keep hearing children pounding up and down the corridors and lights going on and off. Finally, around 4am I do what my mother always did and I say to God: 'If it's to be, it's to be. Over to you.' Another glorious cop-out, but one sufficient to bring sleep.

Tomorrow I'll drive north and wait for the answer. If unlikely, they say they'll accept the offer, well I can always pull out on the pretext of having found another house.

Can't I?

Chapter 8

I AM calm, cool and grown-up. I initial the last page of the interminable 'Promesse de Vente' and shake hands with le maître, the notaire who has read me my rights in French – even though he's clearly bored while Gloria translates the tricky bits.

We are in a surprisingly modern office carved out of the 17th century heart of Auvillar, another of the 'plus beaux villages' of France. It is roughly 15 minutes from Las Molières sitting high above the Garonne, commanding the view for miles over the plains.

The centre, reached through the clocktower gate is a columbaged, cobbled film set of the perfect bastide. The circular, open Grain Hall topped with Gers carved figures. Narrow side-streets weave along to the uncompromising authority of the church and its clutch of ecclesiastical buildings now houses or offices.

Others link up to cross the main road to the more mundane aspects of village life – the tabac, the pharmacy, the restaurants with their snatched pavement spaces for eating in the sun.

The main road winds down to the old port where a row of restored houses, once the homes of wealthy wine and tobacco merchants, sit back from the river's edge. These are handsome bourgoise terraced dwellings keeping themselves ever so slightly away from the dealings above.

Gloria had taken me to see a house here feigning surprise when I said: 'But I can see them. I don't want to be anywhere where I can actually see them. You know that.'

'See what? Golfech?' she asked with the disarming tilt of the head she uses when at her most scheming. 'Oof – we don't even notice them anymore.'

I have to admire her estate agent's ability to have an answer to all objections. For Gloria there are no problems – as she frequently proudly says – only solutions. But even Gloria cannot deny the twin cooling towers of the Golfech Nuclear Power Station lying barely five miles from Auvillar ; their columns of steam a landmark even when the concrete shields are no longer visible. So she has decided that familiarity renders them invisible.

I am not against them for what they represent or the threat they could present. They simply irritate me on aesthetic grounds. I find them unacceptable in such a setting. But the French are pragmatists and 1000 people find work from this site and the towns and villages within range benefit from fistfuls of cash handed over for numerous purposes to keep them sweet and pleased to have this monstrosity in their midst.

From Las Molières and then only from the back of the house can I see the steam. Had there been even the tops of the towers showing through the trees I would not be in this office now signing the first documents towards ownership of my French house.

The notaire, speaking in a sing-song rapid accent, tells me that now I cannot be gazumped, that I have ten days to transfer my five per cent deposit and I can pull out at any stage. The seller cannot.

In front of me is the equivalent of the contentious British purchasers' information packs, paid for by the owner, which gives me details of asbestos (none), lead (a little) and energy output (good). It also points out that because I am buying a house in a hot, clay-based climate, the land can crack and destroy house walls. Gloria quickly interjects that it's only usually a problem when buying new-build. Any cracking in an old house has already happened and settled again. If it were going to fall down, it would have fallen down before now. She smiles, pleased that she's reassured me.

In the commune there is also a risk of flooding, although being at the top of a hill, it is highly unlikely in my particular case. I have read the warnings in all the 'buying in France' books. Torrential rain frequently swells hill and mountain streams into torrents, which sweep away hillsides, overpowering the fosses. Rivers burst their banks without warning and every year there are reports of ruin and death.

'Not here,' says Gloria as I query this. 'No, no, no. We have our own micro-climate. No extremes.' She laughs, patting my arm. 'And you're nowhere near the river.' I initial FC and can feel the treacherous tremor in the arm and leg, which happens when nervous or excited.

I have bought a house in France. For some reason I find myself saying: 'Vonce I had a farm in France,' in the accent Meryl Streep used in the opening of Out of Africa. I say it to myself, not out loud. I say it several times as I gather up the papers, shake the notaire's hand, then Gloria's and even the office secretary on our way out.

Actually I'm not sure whether to tap dance or retch. It has all happened incredibly fast. Only 24 four hours after making it, my offer of £60,000 below the asking price was rejected – with a suggestion that the owner would accept £30,000 above that, lowering the price from £225,000 to £190,000.

The call from Jezza came through just as I was about to leave Le Moulin's car park on my way to Poitou-Charentes and a weekend with Margaret and Bryan. 'No,' I said harder than I intended to. I was hacked off after a disturbed night in the hotel where the children of two Spanish families spent half the night running up and down the corridor. I was cross and anyway still unsure I wanted it. During the long, sleepless night I had again questioned the whole idea of life in the country and thought – hell, no by the time I sat down to breakfast.

'Look I'll go £10,000 more but that is it,' I found myself saying. 'I'm not kidding, that really is it. No more, no deals, no auction.' Once again, unsure of my own judgement, I had thrown it in the lap of the Gods. Ten minutes later she phoned back to tell me it was mine. Oh merde! I arranged to call her on my return to fix the appointment with the notaîre and get things moving.

The drive to St Savin is a particularly lovely one over viaducts, past vineyards, bastide towns positively littering the skyline, but that day I drove almost blind, alternating between fear and euphoria. One minute I felt a new rootedness to this land, a belonging, as I bowled along, the next, a sense of utter alienation.

Driving in to my friends' converted barn, I also realised that I just wanted to speak English and with people who knew me when I was, well, when I was myself is how I thought of it. A glass of champagne was thrust into my hand. Both hugged and congratulated me, but I felt strangely reluctant to pull out the photocopied agency schedule, which showed Las Molières in her starkness. I felt protective of her now.

When I did, it was with the preamble that once I'd done x and y and maybe w, it could, just could be a good house. It wasn't pretty, I admitted, and the photos unfortunately did not do it justice. But I hadn't been stupid, I'd be paying well under the asking price and the most important thing was that all my books would fit.

'For God's sake, Fidelma,' interrupted Bryan with the impatience of the Daily Mail senior executive he once was, 'Just show us the bloody schedule.'

If they were disappointed in my choice, they both hid it so well even under my intense scrutiny, that I found myself becoming enthusiastic and actually excited. Of course it wasn't the maison de maître I'd wanted, nor the edge of a village ivy-clad house, but it had something I told them. I still wasn't quite sure what, which was the problem.

We spent the weekend driving and dining around the area I'd once considered. I no longer wanted to look in immobilers' windows as I was now set on a course. About 20 minutes from their house on a route we'd been before, I suddenly saw a familiar steam cloud and cooling tower. 'I didn't know you had a nuclear power station here?' I said in astonishment. 'Oh that?' said Bryan. 'We never notice it anymore.'

I was still laughing when I drove back to Moissac, Le Moulin and now outside the notaîre's office. 'I think I'm becoming hysterical,' I tell Gloria. 'I think I've made a big mistake.'

'No, no.' (the usual response) 'You've bought a lovely house at a very, very good price. She's a little tired now, but when the French had her, she was beautiful. I know she's a little ugly but she just needs love. Would you like a glass of champagne?'

For once I refuse. I need to phone my world and finally say out loud: 'Vonce I had a farm in France,' to people who would get it. Having come in my own car, I also wanted to drive back to Las Molières and see if it looked different now that I owned it.

I rationalise to myself that this moment was long overdue and I have made a wise choice. I could have spent even more months going in and out of houses, never finding that perfect one, never settling for something I didn't quite like. As a compromise it wasn't bad. I do feel I have betrayed Jean-Louis who tried his best, but I have a new best friend now, Gloria, and well, again, I'll think about that tomorrow.

So I drive through 'my' countryside and turn in to the chain-locked drive. Las Molières is shuttered and sullen again. Sunken into herself, as if the effort to look good that day was far, far too much. Looking too large and alone – lonely even.

Now it is almost mine I allow myself all the bad, dark

thoughts pulsing upwards as I sit here in the dwindling sun. Snakes, wild boar, ticks on the dog, tropical storms rush to the fore, and, my God, is that damp on the walls? How did I miss that green mossy tide and darker line of moisture being sucked from the earth?

I have also lied to my son who still hasn't seen it. The child of an architect he was obviously parroting his father when he asked if I had got a survey. Naturally, I'd said haughtily. Am I stupid? Of course I am, but with reason.

People don't get surveys in France. You can, usually from a semi-retired ex-pat architect or surveyor who will apply British standards to houses which have and never have had foundations. Who will charge a bomb for telling you the obvious - the house is badly plumbed, badly wired, needs a new roof and is damp. The results will be so depressing that certainly at my price, you'd never buy any house here. So what is the point?

Plus when paying cash there is no higher body to re-ask the pertinent questions such as: what is that green mossy tide along the front of the house? Why is the interior paint crumbling? Why do the grounds turn into lakes when it rains? I have never paid cash before so in a way I am utterly dazzled by being able to take a decision all my own.

I went by instinct. It may come back to haunt me, but I have gone by smell and another, less explainable factor. All those weeks gagging on entering houses where damp smothered even the cooking smells. Houses that have dehumidifyers in every room, constantly sucking the moisture from the air. And surely the wet on the outside walls is because of the last rainstorms?

I squint at LM and if this were a film, it would rapidly fast-forward. The rendered walls would be cloaked by ivy, vines and wisteria; a pergola would house a marble-topped table under honeysuckle and clematis and other flowery things whose names I hope to know.

The in-ground pool, now at the front yet to the side of the house, would be silently green awaiting the first shrieks of friends as they lifted themselves from teak deck beds to plunge away the sweat of a 32-degree day. Or perhaps the trickled sound of a lone swimmer counting the lengths in sighing pleasure of being there, simply alone.

Butterflies and bees would flit around strategically placed arbours hiding padded, curved stone seats and tables for two, books and glasses of wine lying awaiting the return of the now refreshed swimmers.

The edges of the fields no longer raw, but clothed in hedging and more trees. A raised vegetable garden would tumble with tomatoes and every conceivable kind of salad leaf. A separate herb garden of sage, rosemary, basil and mint would provide the basics for the effortless open-air meals and salads which would make coming here such a treat for the envious city-trapped friends.

Terracotta pots and giant urns would erupt in vibrant, luscious flowers along terraces and paths lined with lavender bushes, their reclaimed slabs interspersed with planted squares to drape any harshness.

The unattractive plain glass 'patio' doors would be transformed into square-paned true French doors, more large urns guarding either side and as music drifted dreamily through these now-open doors, so would I. Tall, tanned, lithe in some form of whispering kaftan, calm, serene, smiling. Bloody gorgeous in fact and about 20 years younger.

For that moment I can see Las Molières and me in all our potential glory, but it rapidly dissipates as I realise it won't be through the miracle of celluloid. Only hard, hard work will do it as there will be nothing close to the money left to create such a dream out of this unpromising site.

And at this age I doubt I'll grow to the 5ft 11ins of my imaginary height and I certainly couldn't afford the plastic surgeon to scalpel out the new me to go with it. Even if I could it would be a sham, as perhaps would be any attempt to take this unpretentious house to a higher level.

Perhaps I'm coming to this too late, too tired, too jaded, too old. Too alone? When Pierce's father and I took on an old farmhouse in Perthshire we were still in our 30s and I could work a 12-hour day, sometimes more and still have the energy to muck out horses, pull weeds, walk dogs for miles and entertain week-end guests. I even had enough spring in my step to haul myself up on a horse.

But I could also drive away each day to the city knowing child and house were well cared for – a live-in nanny, and a daily housekeeper, overseen by my mother who lived with us and did the cooking. I was, as always, playing at this latest role. This time, this era, the 'having it all,' of newspaper executive by day, hostess and mother at the weekends. Even then I cheated, buying five course meals from The Country Kitchen - wonderful rustic dishes of pheasant and grouse which could be bought from large freezers, all created by Mrs Wilson and her team.

Each time I collected the box with everything from soup to chocolate mousse, Mrs Wilson would run me through the details of how I'd made it, in case some smart-arse guest tested my knowledge. In the end she was even making up my orders in my own crockery for added authenticity.

While I shortcutted and convinced myself I was the star of my own Aga-saga, George had the love, the will and the knowledge to tender to a large organic garden, carve a kitchen from old church pews, log and chop trees, even build a verandah-enclosed tree-house complete with sleeping platform. And, like me, work too.

When one of us was down at the amount of work still to be done or the galloping interest rates, which had our mortgage running at 14 per cent, the other would come up with reassurance or solutions. We could still smile at each other proud of what we'd achieved and were achieving despite the cost in cash and lost sleep. It took less than eight years before we no longer smiled at each other, or had any solutions left either for the house or ourselves.

Such thoughts reminded me of the sheer hard slog needed to keep old farmhouses from settling back into nature, of the odd nights when ,for a variety of reasons I was alone in the house and filled with such superstitious dread and cowardice that walking to the bedroom in the old stable wing was impossible. Nights when, still fully-clothed, I slept fitfully instead on the sitting room sofa, the three dogs around me, the lights and the television mumbling away to drown out the sound of my rational and irrational fears.

Of the nights when the wind was so wild that we lay listening to the tiles flapping a manic, discordant tune – wondering if tonight was the night they flew away forever. Of the number of times towards the end – my mother dead, the boy at boarding school – when I felt the old house almost willing us to go as life and cash drained from it, turning coldly from us disappointed and disgusted at our failure.

And me knowing the time had come to return to the city, hiding away glossy brochures showing kitchens with granite work surfaces, new windows without peeling paint, greedily and privately devouring descriptions of integral appliances, power showers, choice of tiles, curtains and carpets.

Treacherously visiting misnamed penthouses, lofts and split-levels, running hands over smooth edged doors – my mind already on a new single life where plasma screens flattened onto walls and gas fires lit in an almost convincing way at the touch of a remote control. One where coal was not shovelled into a stove, or wood pushed into a fireplace.

A world with only me, my exeat son, one, maybe two dogs, but no hens whose blood stained plumes bid farewell despite tender care; no filthy Wellington boots or silent nights amid the red-marked bills and accusations of carelessness and profligacy. A world of nearby restaurants, bars, friends and home delivery of every ethnic food available. An instant, easy, life with everything on call without effort beyond dialling.

When I slunk home after such after-work brick and mortar infidelities, the Gartloaning farmhouse knew, even if George didn't and she started to shrink away from me as I detached from her and the other living occupant, already planning another, so different, life.

I always think of houses as 'her.' I always think of houses

as individually living entities, which can welcome, reject, or turn against you. Perhaps it's the Irish in me, but I also know from the second I cross a threshold if others still inhabit a house many, many years after they've taken their last breath. My mother had it and my son has it to a lesser degree.

More importantly I know if I'm wanted in a house. Gartloaning had its ghosts, but they saw us as we were then when we crossed the threshold and welcomed us in, in hope for the resurrection of the old shieling. Las Molières has no ghosts, no sly spectres in cold corners, or glimpsed mocking movements. No memories to replay in her stone walls at certain hours.

I felt that the first day I walked in, because that and damp are what I search for. But she, the house herself, ultimately invited me in and now I'm here, her new owner, thinking back too deeply on my last venture into the country and a house that needed more than I could ultimately give it, or want to give it.

What am I trying to prove? In my heart I know I'm only comfortable at first-floor level with doors locked and barred, with perfect kitchens and bathrooms where marble predominates and plumbing is something I just accept and need not ever consider.

Where fires light at the push of a button on a control and other gas is on demand - not in a container - which needs a science degree to replace. Where streetlights penetrate bedrooms, throwing into light relief familiar pieces of furniture, so that when one wakes from the night terrors it is not into darkness.

Where strong footsteps of people going somewhere ring

out below my window, and curses and laughter smash through the silence giving me the consoling balm that I am never alone even if I am. It is a cocooning sound for someone like me. Safe in a most unlikely way.

How can I feel safe here? There's too much of this, too much ... too much... nature. Too much land, dirt, render, sky, trees... and silence. I need noise, life, unnatural city life not this too real life as I've just reminded myself.

Nothing has changed about Las Molières as I've gone through all this in my mind. The sky is darkening and still no birds have sung. But it's all too late now unless I pull out before the ten days are up. If I do that I can never show my face in this part of France again. Certainly not in the column. I am committed to a life turned on a drunken whim, honed on a desire to be different yet, in hindsight, awfully predictable.

I realise I have no plan B. I cannot cast a cold eye and say to myself: 'Nope, not for you. Move on. Let's try... 'Again, let's try where? Once more I prepare to drive away repeating my mantra: 'I can do this,I can do this.' Under the throb of the mantra is the other darker: 'I have to do this.'

Anyway, I rationalise again, it is not as if I will be totally marooned amidst the sunflower fields. Barely two miles away is a large village with three doctors, two vets, two restaurants, a bar, a newsagent, a baker and a butcher, even two hairdressers. Toulouse centre, an hour. And anyway, it's time to stop being so frightened of everything apart from where my job may lead me. I don't have the job any more, remember, so I only have me.

I'm a few years just short of 60, whether I accept it or not.

Time to be wise and steady - to stop seeing ghosts and ghouls, to calmly buy country houses and kiss goodbye to nights in clubs, dancing like the girl who still curls inside me even though horrific cramp moves me to the side-lines after three, literally, breathtaking dances.

To turn into the woman who is the next stage in this life, which plays out to a tabloid tune. To become the woman I never was because I was so busy besting the man next to me. Isn't that the next stage? Is it buggery as far as I'm concerned, but I'll buy into it if it gets me through this. Again, financially, I don't have a choice so I have to turn it into that, as if it is my plan, my aim and as if I have a controlled centre which plots out my course as some sort of heroine of my age.

Gloria has already invited me to join the Cultural Club, in Lavit - 16 euros a year - where they hold art, cookery and dance classes. My heart sinks as I do not and never have wanted to be in a club. But then, what else will I do if I can't earn? How will I fill the hours once dedicated to deadlines? Gloria is 80-odd, but says the others are younger – 70, 60. Can't she see how young I am?

My heart doesn't just sink, it drowns in a deep pool of perceived old age when mentally I'm still 18 and crying for someone to rescue me, but they're all so old they can't swim to my aid. I'm too young for this I scream in my head while smiling my thanks to her.

So I turn it around - as I have no way out as I see it at this moment. In six months I'll be able to cook a perfect omelette aux fines herbes before heading off for a tango with a toothless farmer - or more likely, his wife. I try to think of this as a good thing and a great adventure, another episode in my life, which I can turn into columns or, at the very least, amusing stories for my friends who still live in cities.

As always I make it better than it is. I will write a column suggesting I'm so looking forward to the dancing and the cooking and at the end of it, I'll almost believe I am. Inside I'll be screaming, but already writing the words for the next column, and thinking about how I'll make it a great joke for my friends who just want to hear I'm there.

So I'm here outside the house that's three quarters mine, knowing I won't pull out of the deal. Knowing there are no ghosts or ghouls, only all my fears, which I will have to face once I sign the final papers. Knowing I should not buy this, and knowing it is already too late.

Once more I reverse the car, but this time I don't look back. There's no point now. I head back to the hotel, not even noticing the poppies or the menacing birds of prey, not even looking at Lavit. I'm thinking deliberately of the more promised champagne from the sweet souls who've stood on the sidelines of my solo quest in Le Moulin, no doubt chattering amongst themselves as to my success. I'm touched by their delight as another foreigner arrives.

The further I get from Las Molières, the further the dark thoughts disappear. Gartloaning becomes just one of the many places I've lived in and the name of yet another story to tell of friendly ghosts and lost hopes. I rub out in my mind the fact that when I left her I swore I would never again place my heart in a country setting. I would always know where I was at ease, at peace, at home. The City. Noise, dirt, drunks... life.

Excitedly I lift my mobile to phone and tell my friends: 'Vonce I had a farm in France.'

Chapter 9

IN my sad little head I had decided to stand at the bow of the ship à la Kate Winslet in Titanic as we sailed away from Poole en route to France.

It was to be a private joke and if no one were looking, I might also have croaked a quick chorus of: 'Here, there, wherever etc.,' flinging my arms out in a dramatic farewell.

Instead I end up lurching and clutching the rails at the stern, desperately trying to light my fag on the seventh roll, as, inside, helped by their 7am fried breakfasts, half the passengers are throwing up into sick bags while still sitting in their seats. Some of the bags are full size sacks.

What a day to leave Britain. The worst storms in 40 years predicted and France under a similar threat. Fortunately smokers rarely get seasick because nothing, nothing, stops us from heading to the deck - the best place to be to keep an eye on the horizon and so avoid the disconcerting heaves and swells.

I had reckoned that from Cherbourg to the château

chambre d'hôtes in Poitou-Charentes I had picked as a welcome half-way spot would take roughly five hours on the journey south of around nine and a half hours. I had not of course factored in torrential rain, unconfident driving of my new left-hand drive 4x4 tank and a new fear of overtaking anything in rain, particularly lorries.

In the back of the car, pinned amongst the bin bags of clothes, boxes and documents, Portia lies on rugs and her sheepskin, head lifting occasionally to fix me with mournful brown eyes.

After seven hours of driving I finally reach the outskirts of Poitiers, stopping in a lay-by to give her a break - the pair of us lost, drowned souls under a rapidly darkening sky. Looking at the map in the guidebook it seems relatively simple to find the slip road to the listed house. It should only be ten minutes away.

An hour later having circumnavigated Poitiers a good ten times, snarling in frustration at finding no such road, I pull back into the lay-by and phone the château which was owned, said the book, by a rather eccentric Vicomte and his wife.

In French I beg for help, then ask if they could speak English, as I was so tired I could barely remember my own tongue never mind theirs. The clipped response leaves me in no doubt that I am speaking to Madame, La Vicomtesse herself. 'No I can't,' she said in the clear, strident French vowels of the upper-class. 'Your French sounds more than good enough to me. Use it. We have an English couple also staying and they've already started. We couldn't wait so you'd better hurry up if you want to eat.'

With that she gives instructions, which bear no relation to

the one in the book. I'm not quite sure of some words, but I am not risking her ire by asking her to repeat them. The phone had clicked down anyway.

I head, this time towards Limoges as Portia stands swaying and restless in the back. It is sheer chance we find the village sign and château as I reverse down a back lane ready to return to Poitiers and give up for the night. In front of me is an exquisite chunk of French history - at its heart the main house, a Louis X111 Pavillion, its three-storey tiled roof an elegant pitch. Abutting it a two storey Orangerie. But even in the rain, the formal gardens of box hedging, parterres and avenues, seem oblivious in their precision to the vagaries of the weather.

I have barely stopped when three bustling elderly people, the man holding an umbrella, surround the car with the impatient gestures which signal: 'For God's sake get a move on,' in any language. I am soon to discover this is Le Vicomte, his irritable wife and his sister - the inheritor of the château in some bizarre anomaly of French law.

So tired I practically sway from the car, uttering apologies and explanations which are brusquely discounted as they push me towards the door. 'Vite, vite,' says Madame. 'Dinner is almost over. You must come now.'

Tired and getting wetter, I am a little sharper than I intend. 'No. I'll do without dinner. I must see to my dog first.' I walk past them, opening the boot and she emerges, dignified though jittery, her long nose turning up to sniff her whereabouts. She leaps out bestowing on the trio a look of utter disdain and disinterest before squatting on their perfect lawn, voiding herself with total concentration. Merde, I think, literally, turning to face certain disapproval. Far from it. The trio have stepped back in honour and recognition of a fellow aristocrat. Warm smiles and chirrups of approval transform their pinched features and closed faces. Dinner is forgotten for now and I realise I have gone up several notches with my possession of such a creature.

La Vicomtesse leads us instead to a ground floor suite of gloomy, but darkly beautiful rooms with a choice of chaises-longues 'pour le chien.' The bed is high and over-ornate and rather ominously the cabinets and chairs crowding the room are filled with Edwardian china dolls; their pursed cold lips and unblinking glass eyes seemingly all fixed on the bed itself. Dolls give me Chucky thoughts and once alone in this room I will make sure they are all turned to the wall – eyes closed.

In the simple shower-room off the little private hall I fill Portia's water bowl and empty dried food into another after asking the Lady's permission. 'Of course, of course, we cannot have her going outside in this weather.' After watching Portia drink, with the expression mothers reserve for babies who have just swallowed their first solids, she suddenly unlocks another door in this little self-contained suite.

Smaller than mine, it has a three-quarter bed, topped with antique white linen and several cushions. Another chaise-longue is the resting place for more be-ribboned dolls which she carefully removes to a window-sill. 'I have decided Porrsha (as she pronounces it) should have this room. She'll be more comfortable on the bed or she can have the day-bed. Her choice.'

'Good heavens, no,' I tell her imagining the cushions going flying as Porrsha makes her nest, nudging off the pillows with her nose, pulling back the sheets to crawl

Never come between a woman and her dog.

Almost in harmony... Pierce and me.

The mini stable - one day an outdoor sitting/dining room?

The end of the search... Las Molières beckoned me in.

The kitchen/dining room showing the wood pervert's handiwork.

Cooking before my sang froid left me.

The aftermath of yet another long summer lunch at Las Molières.

Day's end - herding cars fair takes it out of you.

Christmas Eve - the calm before the storm of the fosse septique.

My two great loves - my son, Pierce and my dog, Portia.

Happiness for Pierce is a new toy and 30 tons of gravel.

The Blessed Brian takes a break from the plasterboard.

Portia - free at last!

Oh my God, I'm en France!

inside. She's already eyeing it; I feel her tensing and hold tighter to the lead and collar forestalling any leap on to it. La Vicomtesse shrugs, but leaves the door unlocked.

I bed Portia down in the hall and we finally head to the main house for dinner, where in a large kitchen dining room with glints of delft tiles and ornate candlesticks around an enormous stone carved fireplace, a silent, rather sweet looking, middle-class English couple are chewing in a definite state of shock.

Across the hall in the kitchen proper, the sister is obviously dealing with the meal herself, aided by the old Viscount whose back and tentative movements exude a touching combination of a desire to help and an ignorance of how to. There is an air of 'old glory' here - asset rich, but cash poor; of a trio bound in service to a family house, forced to take in paying-guests to stave off flogging the family silver or worse.

I am shoved in front of a very tartly dressed salad of several leaves, and told to hurry it for my meat. The English couple introduce themselves and in quiet voices, while looking across the hall where voices are now raised, ask where I've come from. Before I can answer, La Vicomtesse grabs the plate of salad, which was barely edible and I'm faced with well, meat. I think it is a piece of chicken, and a slice of pork with a gherkin on top. Madame returns with a beautiful, though tarnished, silver bowl full of peas. 'From our garden,' she says, shovelling them on to my plate, cutting right across the English couple.

Between the pair is an almost empty bottle of wine. Perhaps a quarter left. At this stage I'm ready to kill for it, but the bottle is not pushed towards me and my wine glass stays empty as I try to better define what I'm eating. Worse still the couple have each got a practically full glass in front of them from which they occasionally take a tiny sip.

I don't want to ask either the couple or the Viscountess for wine. Perhaps it is wine they've brought. Perhaps it is one bottle per table. Perhaps I'll look a lush if I grab the bottle and pour the remnants into my glass. I play with my glass as our host and hostess hover in the background, praying they will notice that my hand is clutched around – horror of horrors - an empty wine glass and the mute plea of 'hello, I'm eating? No wine?'

Nothing. I try chatting again to the couple to be immediately interrupted by the Lady who is blatantly ignoring them in only speaking French. I give up on both hope of wine and conversation. Looking again around the room I catch sight of hunting photographs and oil paintings of green liveried men and women hunting with hounds. Women in tri-cornered hats sitting side-saddle on well-groomed hunters.

Finally, we have a common purpose and I admit my Irish heritage of hunting, flinging in names like 'The Kilkenny' and 'The Galway Blazers,' old famous hunts. In that instant I become worthy of attention and La Vicomtesse, a once and still beautiful woman of possibly 70, desperate to light on a kindred soul, drops her resistance and becomes a hostess of choice.

Her eyes lose their irritable flash and suddenly shine showing the clamped down intelligence of a brain once used for finer moments than waiting on the flotsam, probably loathed and needed in the same measure, which washes up at this house.

'Up, up,' she cries, ushering me to the other end of the table swiping the almost empty bottle from underneath the noses of the couple who keep smiling in a nervous desperate parody of good English manners under all provocation. Her husband, dressed in the English fashion in old, but beautifully cut tweeds, his silver hair pin-pointing an age difference of several years between them, winks rather charmingly at her as if in on some joke.

She positions me carefully directly under a massive beam, so broad I feel it could hold the whole weight of the house by itself and, praise the Lord, she pours me the last drops of the wine.

Quite frighteningly transformed into a pair of indulgent parents, they tell me, taking turns in very beautiful almost lyrical French that anyone who drinks the last of a bottle of wine underneath this special beam will be married within a year. Obviously they have judged my ringless finger, my devotion to my dog and my solitariness as indicative of a desperate want of marriage.

In not very beautiful French I raise my empty glass and tell them: 'Unless he has a title, a château like this, disgustingly rich with no children, hopefully widowed and impotent... not a bloody chance.'

Well in my head I tell them. Outwardly I laugh and say: 'Oh non, non, non.' I'm far too tired to tackle anything like the above and get it right. The English couple who are following little if any of this, judging by their fixed smiles, decide to retire. 'Fine, goodnight,' says the Lady barely giving them a glance while motioning me up from the chair saying: 'Come to the salon. We'll have an Armagnac and chat further.'

Into a corridor where I stop to look at more hunt photographs, these of her daughter, this of herself many years ago, this the meet last year, I'm very aware of the cold seeping out from stone walls stoically bereft of heating. The salon itself, once grand has not only the smell of damp, but inner tidemarks, huge dehumidifiers placed in corners. I don't want to stare too obviously, but among some fine furniture and heavy gilt framed oils there are spaces showing where pieces and paintings have been removed bit by bit, year by year.

Over the next couple of hours and coffee and Armagnac she tells me of the history of the château, the disputes within the family, the difficulties of keeping the place going and gives no quarter to my French or my tiredness. I have asked her to correct me, which she does frequently, giving me a lesson both in received pronunciation as we would call it and I suppose 'U' and 'Non-U' words. Always say parfois rather than quelquefois for sometimes; always use the full Mesdames and Monsieurs when entering or leaving a shop, never M'dames, M'sieurs, and never, ever pick up an accent.

She wants to know if my house is pretty and seems disappointed when I tell her no. She is hungry for all she can draw from me and tell me and although it is all a little odd I am enjoying her directness, her clever eyes and her almost girlish need for information. At one point her husband comes in to see if we want more coffee and is prompted by her to re-tell the history of his family. He does this proudly before backing out shyly smiling at his wife, content she has someone to talk to.

But the dog is alone in a strange hall after a confusing journey; my French is getting more limited by the second and so we wish each other goodnight shaking hands with a rather touching formality.

I walk Portia around the grounds, picking up after her, stowing the mess in its plastic bag in the back of the car for ditching tomorrow. Back in the room I close every curtain, turn the dolls' faces to the wall, cover one chaise-longue with her blanket before she can jump on it, and fall asleep with a light burning in the corner.

I awake with her beside me on the bed and the sound of more rain battering the long windows. After dressing I re-open the dolls' eyes and turn them back to the room; replace the cushions flung over the floor by Portia's night meanderings trying every day bed before leaping up on mine. This time I put her straight into the car after our sodden walk alongside my re-packed bag and go in for breakfast.

La Vicomtesse greets me with fresh delight, much to the surprise, I can see, of the English couple, apparently still bewildered by simply being in the realm of this capricious woman. We murmur the familiar pleasantries of 'sleep well?' 'weather still dreadful,' 'where are you off to today?' until their coffee pot is now snatched from them as the Lady pours me a cup, entreating me to croissants and bread, lifted away as well.

Immediately she launches into another series of questions to me. 'Where's Porssha? Ah. Did you walk the big avenue? Good.' Her back is firmly turned on Mr and Mrs Keep Smiling Whatever Happens. I'm embarrassed, but decide there is nothing I can do. Now she draws a chair up beside me and slowly, but very earnestly tells me that life is often a moment when the page turns. It is a very French expression. 'You meet someone out of the blue when you are not expecting it and you feel a connection.

'I've met you as your page has turned. It is fate – kismet and I know I will be forever in your life.'

Her intensity should disturb me, but it doesn't. I know my page has turned, but I could not have put it so eloquently. She gestures behind her and turns away from the still frozen couple: 'Not like these people. So ordinary.' I pray they don't understand a word, but the gesture is again universal and I fear they do.

She disappears to return with a large Hermès ashtray; clutches my hands and ask me permission to give me the three kisses (bisous) 'You'll come back for the first meet, as my friend, not as a paying guest. And promise me you will write to me? Remember for you the page has turned.'

I feel very touched if a little baffled by it all. Now she is handing me stiff, small personal cards. 'Here,' she points, 'are people you should know in your region. Not many,' she sniffs again, 'but then that's your area for you. They're the right sort, the people you really need to meet and when they see my card you'll be welcomed.'

As I drive away she is still watching me before she wraps her cashmere shawl around her bony shoulders, and nose in the air a little similar to Portia, she has a final sniff before turning back inside.

I drive a little while before pulling over to peer at the cards. There is no Marquis, but there is a Comte.

The rain lashes us all the way down the auto-route, but I keep thinking of la page turning and decide La Vicomtesse is an omen for good, hopefully a precursor to many more interesting days and nights. We stop just once, at a service station and turn off for Lavit on the final 20km through the fruit farms, the trees bent and miserable looking, unused to such weather in June.

Lavit is even quieter than usual for 4.30 in the afternoon. There are lights in the bar and the newsagents, but a large sign announces that the only mini-supermarket, 8 à Huit, is closed for two weeks for repairs. As I pull up outside the estate agent's I see parked cars with dents the size of tennis balls pockmarking their surface. Tarpaulin flaps over several roofs. I feel my semi-euphoric mood evaporating.

I've never seen the flat I'm to stay in for the ten days until I sign the Compromis de Vente and take over the keys. At the price Gloria's charging me I'm not expecting a penthouse, but it has been a holiday let so should be fine. She greets us with genuine delight and the double-kiss immediately dubbing Portia Mademoiselle Lavit, because 'She is a beauty queen,' then hustles us through a back door into a dark hall where a narrow staircase reaches into a black unknown.

On this level there is a sitting room lit by a dim bulb leading to a verandah with stairs into a small yard with scrub grass. 'You'll come in and out this way,' she says, as I notice the magazines have dates from many years back. With slow footsteps we follow her up the main stairs into what should have been a landing, but now houses a battered, thin sofa and chair; an old box television on a stand and a coffee table. To the left, a kitchen with an oil-cloth covered table and chairs, a door out to a covered verandah with a similar set up. All is clean, but dingy and shabby in the low-level main lights, casting depressing shadows.

To the right, a bedroom with windows over the square. The bed is unmade and she pulls out nylon multi-coloured sheets for me to fit later. There is water penetration in a corner of the room and she tells me: 'We had a hailstone storm. Hailstones so large that they've destroyed the supermarket roof, cars, house roofs and even killed cattle in the fields. Terrible, terrible.' We move to the bathroom, a mirror-image of two-star utilitarianism. I feel the panic rising of being stuck here. More steps lead to an attic and another mezzanine bedroom, but I don't want to see there... ever.

I just want to bundle Portia back into the car and drive away fast. Go home. How can I turn on my heel and offend this woman who has hand-held me through this whole process? So I smile instead and wearily go back downstairs to unload my bags and the bin bag of Portia's bowls and familiar toys.

Now alone, I walk through the place switching on lights that either barely register or don't come on and make up the bed in its swirling orange and brown synthetic clothing. There is not even a loo roll in the place, the restaurant is shut tonight and the supermarket shut down. It is Monday and few places are open but there is Beaumont 14 kms away, so back we go into the car.

I make the mistake of detouring to see my house again. Never a coup de coeur, but I had convinced myself in my absence that it could be made beautiful. Not this late afternoon. Las Molières is back to just a chunk of ugly stone in the middle of nowhere. In keeping with my mood, or because of it, even the surrounding fields are suddenly mis-shapen, the enchanting forests of the last visit, threatening and overpowering. Two cars pass me, drivers and passengers , dark heavy browed faces staring out with what feels like malevolent scowls.

Heartsick, I go on to Beaumont picking up the basics, plus dog food, ham, bread, butter and two bottles of red for I fear it is going to be a long night. We pick our way into the flat through the cat-fouled back yard, up the tricky steps and on and up to the cold, miserable kitchen. Portia pads around as I fill her bowl with the cheapest food that's ever crossed her allergy-prone lips, doubting she'll touch it and I'll be back to coaxing her with hand-held mouthfuls of salmon and mince to keep her upright.

I'm shivering as much from displacement as unseasonal cold as I look at my pathetic black bin-bags now stacked in the half-sitting room. I am not a weeper - I only cry at ludicrously sentimental moments in films when the dog or the whale dies or the horse gives it all in the last furlong and then dies.

So I am shocked when out of me comes the harsh, grunting sounds of misery and I realise that tears truly are hot. And I am crying - non-stop, full strength tears; gut-wrenching, horrible, snottery, violent explosions of unstoppable anguish. I barely notice that Portia has eaten everything in her bowl and sloped off to the thinning sofa to stretch herself along it in silent contentment.

Ever since I was a little girl, flight has been the answer to my problems. Run, run, when in trouble or scared. Literally, when seeing a chimney on fire in Guard Carroll's house in Kilkenny, Ireland; pedalling on my three-wheeler as fast as my four-year-old legs could take me. Mentally, into books, or behind closed doors, phone unanswered when uncertain of the next move in a mercurial professional or personal life.

I hate confrontation. I retreat. My life has been spent often alone. A gregarious recluse, content in my own company, but delighted to party when asked or giving; a compulsive phone chatterer, but equally snug with the rain against the windows, a glass of wine, a fag and a compelling new book.

I've been fortunate in that loneliness is a stranger to me. Looking back it seems I have been lonely only twice. This is the second time. The first time was on arriving in Glasgow from England aged 22 with digs in an old lady's house in suburban King's Park where I was shown to a high bed and taken to 'my' Victorian sitting room with an Aspidistra the focal point in the bay window.

Venturing out to my job at the Daily Record, I encountered one-legged beggars and three-legged dogs and people who rasped at me with an aggressive tongue, which I couldn't understand. Nightly I whinged on the large black, bakelite phone to those back home, bereft of anyone who loved me and lost in an alien world of knowing looks and people with families to return to at the end of the day.

It was also the first time I cried on the phone – sobbing, silence, sobbing. My mother absorbed it at first and finally told me to pack the suitcases my colleagues had given me at the Evening Gazette, Blackpool, with which to 'travel the world' and come back. She was sure I could get back my job and my bedroom was waiting. Or, or, I could stiffen my backbone, stop the snivelling and get on with it.

Her harsh words cracked my self-pitying monologue. I could hardly breathe hearing her say such things and I hung up feeling I was now totally on my own. My own mother had deserted me.

Down the hall, my landlady was filling a stone hot-water

bottle for my high bed and I could see her look of triumph that she now had me to herself. The blackness rushed over me.

Later I discovered that my mother was herself in tears having to deliver such hard words to me. But knowing me she knew she had to do so to make me survive, continue my life and fill me with steel.

Bent over this oil-cloth table under the gloomy light, slurping red wine and clutching my mobile, I fantasise about phoning her number. Of course she is long dead, but I wonder if I could remember our old house phone number then maybe she would pick it up and hear me crying again on the line. And maybe she would tell me to 'stiffen my backbone,' and 'get on with it.' And maybe I could tell her that I was a little lost, in France and not sure any more about how I'd got here and why. Even though I was middle-aged and a mother myself.

And then maybe she would tell me to pack 'those' bags and come home. And this time I would. I could come home now because I had nothing to prove. And I really wanted to come home. But I couldn't remember her number, so I phoned everyone who was in my mobile address book instead.

None of my friends had ever heard me like this. Barely comprehensible, barely vocal. Telling them I'd made the most disastrous mistake of my life. Actually sobbing. Hardly responding to their calm, kind, rather frightened voices. Hardly hearing the ones who were prepared to reschedule their lives to fly out to where I was. I even said: 'I'm lonely,' to them, disgusted at my weak words.

I never do lonely or loneliness. I'm appalled at myself and

decide to stop phoning, exhausted, helped by the almost finished bottle of wine. I go downstairs, let Portia out into the backyard, swaying slightly at the door. She quickly comes back and I switch out the lights, semi-falling into the bedroom.

The lamp outside gives a glow similar to the street lights in Glasgow, so I have no need of a side-light. I feel quite comforted and Portia stretches out below the bed. Curving into myself, I sleep.

Chapter 10

IN the end it's a straightforward choice. You swim or you drown and ultimately I'm a swimmer, so I have kicked out hard and fast to get on with it all. After last night, a night of despair, there was only one way to go - up.

And so, red-raw eyes hidden behind sunglasses, grateful that it is no longer dark and the rain has stopped, I clipped the lead on Portia and headed for lunch at the restaurant in the square. Time moves to a different rhythm in rural France. From noon to two, sometimes three, everything closes as lunch is celebrated. Those who live more than 15 minutes away eat in the bistro, the rest go home, combining a freshly prepared meal with a half-hour siesta.

The offices still, the phones stop ringing, even the birds congregate as one on the power lines, settling in to each other in peaceful silence. There is a wonderful sense of release in the knowledge that there is no point worrying about all the people one needs to contact – the electrician, the cabinet maker, the garden man and the estate agent. For all are incommunicado during this period.

And so, for two lovely, long hours one can simply sit and stare at nothing, for little passes the square as it slumbers in today's 28 degrees. All is calm and silent. My heart slows, my brain stops twirling with its endless questions and I simply 'be.' Yesterday's rain and the shabby flat is forgotten. I feel ashamed of my weepings and wailings of the night before.

For roughly £8 I can order a three course meal and as much wine as I want from the day's fixed menu. The courses are good, though huge, involving chicken, beef, pork , salads or charcuterie. Workmen sit at the other tables sipping wine and water, mopping up their plates with hunks of bread.

Portia and I sit outside although we could be inside and no one would turn a hair, even when I lit up. She is my ice-breaker, welcome in every shop much to her obvious startled astonishment.

Afghans are rare in France, particularly in villages on a route to nowhere and so even the most gimlet-eyed old women melt into smiles and cross to coo to her and then to me. Women who ordinarily could take weeks, probably months to unbend and acknowledge me.

With the excessive politeness bordering on disinterest bred into the French, not one of the handful who have come to inspect the dog ask me any personal questions. But as these are to be my new neighbours and in my craven desire to integrate, I find myself babbling – telling them I have come here to live, out near Balignac you know. I'm not English either, which usually seems to please these people, and by the way, I do apologise for my French, but I am trying.

They look a little shocked at this mad woman, nod every so often, but say or ask nothing in return. It is a definite one-sided conversation. They do keep chatting to Portia, telling her how welcome she is, how beautiful. Even more extraordinarily, she melts back, entranced apparently by their soothing, low in throat endearments; allowing them to pet and admire her.

Normally she'd be backing off, appalled at such intimacies, choking herself in her collar to get away. Here she stretches her beautiful blonde body underneath the table, lazily raising her head for chunks of the chicken, too much for me, but fine for a family of three.

She is eating more at one go than she has ever done in her life having had very little desire for food from being a pup – a common trait in some Afghans. She is not even nibbling neurotically at her fur and I decide to stop the numerous pills given to cope with her various allergies. I think she has actually gone native, settling into this life with an ease and speed I can only envy and hope to emulate. So native I'm sure that if I asked for wine in her water bowl she would sip it and sigh with pleasure. Thank God, one less thing to fret about.

As the week before the final signing rushes on I am so glad to have her by my side, a mute, but caring companion as my emotions ride a roller-coaster. My dark night of the soul is well and truly past, but in the space of a few hours I can go from absolute certainty that I have done the right thing, to dark forebodings of doom and gloom. My friends back home must feel on the same fairground ride as they never know which voice will answer their calls.

I can become quietly tearful watching the spectacular sunsets and sniffle at midnight hearing the toll of the church bells and imagining my coffin rolling in like Little Jimmy Brown. Bong. Piaf's version naturally blaring over the line of black-clothed crones accompanying me on my final journey in this foreign land.

Night-times are the worst when there's nowhere left to go except the dismal flat, my face peering from the window at the few teenagers who loiter in the square eating pizza, yabbering on mobiles.

But my days are semi-filled with setting up the structure I'll need. At the Credit Agricole I have a meeting with a blonde, 40-something bank manager. She is wearing cropped trousers, kitten heels and a black T-shirt with, in English, 'No Excuses' picked out in sequins. Given my past financial history it is not a hopeful sign, but then there is little hope in French banks where loans and overdrafts are only infrequently given after a grilling, which leaves no manoeuvring of the kind I used with such awesome results in the past.

I remind myself that the large salary I flashed in bank managers' faces to convince them of my ability to pay, no longer exists and looking at this woman's lived in face and knowing eyes, I realise I would never, ever have got round this one.

Another day I sit in an immaculate and minimalist office to insure my house and contents, a legal requirement before it's officially mine. She needs to measure the house and so we drive in convoy, Gloria's grandaughter Vanessa taking me and keys to open the house for the first time since my offer was accepted.

Watching her jiggle with the bolts and re-evaluating the bars, I ask why it has so many locks and padlocks.

'It was broken into - twice,' she admits.

My God. 'But your grandmother told me this area doesn't have criminals or crime,' I say, hearing my voice rise. Unwittingly I have used the sort of words one uses to describe organised crime on a Mafia level.

She laughs. 'It's not Chicago. It's because it was a holiday home – opportunistic thieves from Toulouse. Gypsies.' I will learn that every crime is always down to the Gypsies, who, if you believe all you're told, sweep through the country like bandits of old.

Finally the bolts are off and I flinch as we enter, now overwhelmingly convinced I've bought a pig in a poke. Maybe I have. With the torrential rain and hailstones that hit the South last month and the sudden realisation that I have no guttering, I smell and see the dreaded damp. I was buying this house almost purely on the grounds that there was no damp, no smell.

There is now, accompanied by brown stains on the wall, saltpêtre where wall and floor meet. Remembering the room-freshener smell in what will be my bathroom I head for it, revolted by the trio of large black beetles crawling across the adjoining bedroom floor. Spiders have colonised the glass doors, accumulating a larder of flies and centipedes. I am hit by the damp in the bathroom and immediately see the brown marks on the inner wall, opening the cheap cabinet to inhale even deeper damp. No wonder the builder friend would arrive first to open up, quickly painting over the damp, opening windows and spraying to ensure all seemed well.

Again I just want to run. Vanessa sees my face. 'It's nothing,' she soothes. 'All French houses are like this after heavy rain. You've got a good buy, don't worry.' Her grandmother has trained her well. Meanwhile, the insurer is pacing out rough measurements with giant strides and outstretched arms. I do not tell her I will be ripping out most of the bars after she estimates a sum a quarter of what I would have paid in Glasgow.

Anyway it's too late now. Everything I possess is in a truck and on its way from Glasgow. Tomorrow I sign the final Acte, get the keys and pick up Pierce from Toulouse Airport. He is coming for two weeks to help me settle in. Joy of joys. He hasn't seen the house and frankly I'm dreading his reaction, particularly now there most certainly is damp. He also has to spend a night at the flat – at least I've warned him.

'How was it?' he asks in the very, deep manly tone he adopts these days when I phone him to check arrival times. 'Well, after all the rain, obviously a touch of damp,' I say in as casual a manner as possible. 'Mmm. Well at least with the survey we know it's not a major problem. Good job you did that.'

'Mmm...' is my reply.

I uncork the red, take a slurp for courage as all the lights blow in the flat's kitchen. It doesn't even faze Mademoiselle Lavit. She eats her cheap orangey tin of meat in one go and slides off to her sofa. I slam another bit of ham on bread, take it and the bottle next to her and try to watch a game show on the TV. If I close one eye and tilt my head slightly I can just make out the contestants through the blizzard of the old set. A couple of hours later I give up and once more totter to my orange and brown bed.

Back at the notaire's the next morning, there is more

formal signing, ending again in the handshakes. Numerous sets of keys are handed to me and I now have a house in France. It's almost an anti-climax I decide, even though my leg is jumping again and I feel ever so slightly sick. Gloria, of course, promises I will never regret it, offers to take me for a glass of champagne even though we both know it will eat into her precious lunchtime and siesta, so I decline, to leave for the airport and the problems ahead.

I see him before he sees me. Distracted, irritated, eyes fixed on baggage point No. 4, momentarily arrested by the pretty, skinny brunette, no doubt awaiting a lover, he finally acknowledges the small woman with the fixed smile and the big dog dragging her across the marble hall. On hind legs, Portia gives him the deux bisous. 'See? Portia has gone native,' I joke.

'Hello mum,' he says in that quizzical tone, graciously bending to do the same. 'What a f*****g flight. How do people do this? I'm starving. God I hate easyJet. Who are these people? My head's pounding - I need food, fast.'

The pulse is flicking in my temple. 'Yes, Pierce. I'm fine. Got the keys, feeling good. No, no problems,' I reply to his retreating back. He turns, giving a mock shame-faced grin. 'Oh, yeah. Alright? Good. Knew you would be. Vive la France and all that, eh?'

On the journey back with him driving. (Why haven't I washed the car? What's that noise from the engine? Haven't I noticed it pulls badly to the right? When did I last get it serviced? The tyre pressures are definitely off. Don't I care about the car?)

Clinging to the door as we flip round corners I finally yell: 'No I couldn't give a merde about the car so long as it goes and I can see out of the windscreen. What does it all bloody matter?'

'Stressed are we dear?' he replies, a side-long smile of reaction triumph. I realise how truly stressed I am when I want to smash his head with the large Michelin guide lying in the passenger side pocket. I once did beat him about the head on a detour over the Yorkshire Moors, which ended in a screaming frenzy. But that's another story.

In the silence that follows my outburst we pull into Lavit. 'Christ,' he mutters. 'Not exactly heaving, is it?' I know that, but I don't need to be told. 'Let's see the house,' he says.

Oh God no.

'Come on.'

I point out the road and we arrive at the cross-roads to look at it. There is an awful silence. We drive on even though it is almost dark. 'You need to see it with the shutters open,' I say curtly. 'She's not looking her best. We'll come back tomorrow when the sun is out.'

I'm aware of his silence. 'F**k me,' he finally utters. My heart sinks. 'Is that our land?' I'd forgotten how acquisitive my boy is.

'Yeah... goes on and on. Loads of possibilities, but you'll see it all properly tomorrow.'

More silence. I truly resent that I care about this boy's opinion when all my life I've striven to be only myself and needed to please nobody. 'Actually, I quite like it in a strange way,' he tells me. I bloom, blossom, want to hug him, but wait, for the killer thrust that always comes after the compliment.

'F*****g ugly though.' I know that, I don't need to be told. 'Believe me, I've seen worse,' I say, telling him to turn around and let's get back to the really ugly, like where he's staying the night. Half-way down the hill he is trying hard. 'I like this, I like this,' he says, pointing to the maize fields and the farms. 'God, after London this air is amazing. Don't you feel better here already? Think how healthy you'll be here.'

I fling the fag end out of the window. I'd warned him about the flat and expect an explosion. Instead, he takes it in his silent stride, commandeering the bed because of his height and bad back and asking where we are going for dinner. I point at the restaurant through the bedroom window.

As we sit outside the restaurant in the deserted square where the night air is still warm and the night-lights make a pretty picture at ours and the adjoining tables, he raises his glass after an unexpectedly good steak and frîtes.

I've filled him in as to the past few days and he's deeply impressed with the new Portia now lying happily between us. The Vicomtesse story amuses him and we discuss the attributes his forthcoming step-father must have. Strangely, his list coincides exactly with my own.

'Well, this is it now,' he says with an almost contented grin. 'So, bonne chance and all that. Can't wait to see inside the house tomorrow. Bit worried about the smell of damp though. The survey would've shown up any real problems, so I'm not particularly worried about that.'

I quickly suggest an Armagnac before facing back to the flat. He latches on to my evasion faster than the turn of a Venus flytrap sensing a fly. 'Mum? You did get a survey didn't you? Mum?'

I pause a split-second too long. Snap. 'You didn't, you bloody didn't, did you? Admit it. I know you didn't. I can see it in your face.'

'It doesn't work the same way in France,' I explain lamely, relying on the arriving brandy to pacify him as his dummy once did. 'If you commissioned surveys you'd never, ever buy a house anywhere in France. Damp is part of life here. The secret is to make sure it's not too much damp.' My explanation sounds even feebler out of my mouth than in my head.

We stare at each other as somewhere cicadas whirr and the perfume from the flower baskets pulses around us and intermingles with the garlic from the kitchen. It is a really beautiful night. A holiday night - a very French night.

'Merde,' says Pierce.

I sigh in relief that that is all he has to say.

Chapter 11

I T doesn't take long to re-fill the black bin-bags the next
morning, walk the dog, wake the boy, strip the bed and
pack the car for the journey to my new home. By the
time we have covered two of the four kilometres to Las
Molières, we are both spitting vitriol at each other - him
because of lack of food, me because he has predictably
picked a fight.

We are back to the subject of the survey. Back and forth.
Question, response. Nip, nip, nip. I am already wound up,
dreading the truth to come and wrench the car to a stop at
the edge of the fosse. Portia raises a head then settles down
again - she's seen and heard it all before.

The heavy Michelin atlas wallops his arm. I surprise and
shock myself often with my strength and anger towards
this boy.

'You're off your bloody head,' he yelps, grabbing the atlas
from my hands. 'Listen to yourself.'

'Of course I'm off my bloody head,' I yell back. 'Who

could blame me? I'm 56 years old, up a single lane in bloody rural France going to an ugly bloody house I've spent too much on. No job, no money, no bloody life. And, and, all you can bugger on about is the bloody survey.'

We sit a few further seconds in silence before I re-start the car climbing onwards to LM. In silence, we turn in to the drive. In silence, I unlatch the various padlocks, turn keys, turn handles. Las Molières is open to inspection.

We walk through it in further silence. I explain every room in staccato defensive bursts, avoiding his eyes as he picks up every ugly or suspect element. He knocks knowingly on walls – the way I did in front of the English builder – and I know he hasn't a clue either. So I sigh and his face tightens. He sniffs the damp and an eyebrow raises. He inspects the wood pervert's handiwork and mutters away to himself. I know any minute now he'll be outside on his mobile and I'll hear: 'Dad, you won't believe...'

And I'll want to run outside like an angry child and kick his shins.

'Bonjour, anybody home?' We both start at the men who have arrived and quickly unmould our scowling, mean faces into some semblance of sane welcome. Brian and Paul were expected. They have come recommended from the French estate agent. Both are English, but registered and apparently accepted by the French who would not be able to touch the house until a year's time.

I know they feel the tension as Pierce and I shake hands with them. He attempts to assume control by listing the work he instantly sees needs to be done and I hear the euros hitting jackpot. My eyes and squared shoulders warn them that I'm the one in control, the one with the money. Brian is a small, squat man with a Midlands accent and the wide smile of someone who desperately wants to be liked. Paul, in a leather jacket, clutching a portfolio of his work, is an East-End London cheeky chappie who is desperate to impress.

He is here to give me a devis, a quote for the bookcasing which is vital. Brian is the electrician and general all-round tradesman. We walk through the house and I show Paul the walls I want my books on. He wants to show me his photographs of what he has already done. I just want him to measure and price. At this moment, it's all I care about.

Pierce is pointing to walls and roofs and discussing covering them all. I realise that perhaps I want them covered too, but that is up to me, not him. I hear him and the men groaning and laughing. I feel for my house and at this moment I'm ready to cry as I see their sideways glances at each other at this place I now own.

Instead I hit Pierce over the head as he is telling them we need plasterboard, drains, guttering and of course, the major salon on the first floor underneath the hanger. 'I'll decide what we need,' I shriek. 'What I need. Not you.'

I feel the bile burbling as these three pairs of male eyes look on me, the mad woman.

Paul and Brian catch each other's eyes, understand and look away. Brian, teeth gleaming, clasps my upper arms and tells me: 'Look, it's always hard on the first day. I'll come back tomorrow when you've settled down and we'll talk about it then.'

Pierce is rubbing his head and muttering that I'm off mine. The bile is in my throat. 'I hate it,' I spit through my

153

teeth. Paul stares into the distance. Brian says soothingly: 'It'll all look different in the morning. Remember, there are no problems, only solutions. And that's what we're here for.'

It must be a common platitude here.

They scuttle away together no doubt wondering what the hell they've let themselves in for. We stand and stare after them and go to sit on the picnic bench left by the previous owners. The sun, the mellow sound of the birds and the gentle miles-stretching landscape gradually thaw the coldness between us and I feel the tightness go out of my head.

Pierce sighs almost contentedly and we start amicably and adultly to discuss what needs to be done. I agree, depending on cost, that we'll plasterboard most of the ceilings and over the walls where the planks run riot. Paint white all but the massive oak beams in most rooms. He decides to have the room upstairs as his bedroom, not the one in the wing with the bathroom next door. He cannot see beyond the animal stalls and covered-up manger. With the bookcasing, the down lighting and now screeds of plaster-boarding, I doubt there'll be anything much left to do to my grand upper-drawing room.

I rationalise to myself that to have any chance here I must be comfortable in my surroundings and even if it takes every last centime, then it'll have to be done. This was not the plan. This was not the new sensible way forward. Old dogs, new tricks came to mind.

By the time we come back from lunch to await the removal men, we are both quite jolly, not just from the mid-day rosé, but in anticipation of seeing our furniture again.

I used to pride myself on my bohemian attitude to the possessions, saying disdainfully that all I cared about were my books. But my time in the Wiltshire cottage disproved that when I realised I was craving to have my things around me again.

Two enormous attached vans trundle to a halt at the entrance to the drive and I see the look of resigned horror on the two men's faces as they realise they will have to carry everything up the pocked tarmac. At the price this has cost me they should be ferrying it up the Zambezi.

Very rapidly the terracotta tiles in the kitchen disappear under a sea of goods. First in is my elm table and hyacinth reed chairs. The men aren't the slightest bit fazed when I rush to kiss the table, running my hands over its smooth surface and into the knot holes. They are not even remotely disconcerted when I hug my sofa and tell it: 'I've missed you so much.' Didn't even flicker when I roll on my Moroccan carpet showing the Tree of Life, just stopping short of licking its fibres.

'My mother's a bit off her head at the moment,' Pierce tells them matter-of-factly. 'Seen it all before,' says Chic from Aberdeen with the dead-eyed look of a man who truly has – and then some.

Portia is behind the paned-glass door in the hall, staring intently at the goings-on. I'm sure she recognises that Lynedoch Street has come to France and soon she'll be stretched out on the kelim stool, which already sits in front of the wood-burner. In Glasgow it was in perfect proportion to the drawing room - here it looks like a single-bed, dominating the small sitting room, only inches from the equivalently suddenly over-sized sofa.

A mattress goes upstairs to Pierce's room along with the desk and chair for the study. My bed is assembled in the room off the sitting room, the two suede covered kist bedside tables beside it. Portia is removed to the bathroom as crate after crate is put into the holding pen the guest-bedroom has become. There are 45 packing cases of books alone starting to stack up there, almost blocking out the light from the windows – as do rugs, mirrors, wardrobe-cases of clothes with nowhere yet to go. Paintings in crates stack up in the kitchen and boxes of chandeliers, fake crystal, brass and wrought iron add to the turmoil.

As dusk falls the men bring in the final box and call it a day. Tomorrow they're to unpack and put-away, but I will not be getting my money's worth as there really is no-where to unpack to. We have no wardrobes, no bookcases, and hardly any cupboards in the kitchen, or actually, anywhere. Plus there is little point in covering any surface considering the amount of work to be done. They ask to take a shower and tell me they'll be sleeping in the van.

We have to go out again for dinner so naturally we take them with us. Portia we leave lying on the sofa, her head barely raising as I tell her to mind the house as we feel our way out in the dark. She has wolfed down another enormous meal and apparently couldn't give a damn where she is.

Both removal men are cleaner and fresher than we are. The hot water didn't extend to four, but we discover a similar thirst for the pichets of rouge and I wonder what the others in this bistro make of our unlikely foursome. The wine unleashes Chic's broad tongue and we hear of a wife long gone, a life lived on the road, an unjudgemental approach to those brought into new life. Gravely he tells me he thinks I have a good house in comparison to many he's seen and recounts taking a couple from an Edinburgh New Town Georgian house to a rickety pile in the Herault.

'He couldn't stop smiling showing us each room to put the stuff,' he remembers. 'She looked ready to cry and by the state of her had been crying for some time. I wouldn't have taken it as a gift, but you don't know why they've gone there from what they had. You can only guess.'

His big hand grabbed at the glass and he gulped back the last of his red, putting it down with the certainty of a man who has no illusions left. I suggest one for the truck back at the house.

We sit - them on crates, us on the two chairs not covered with bits and after several nightcaps, walk outside to drunkenly wave them goodnight as they retire to their beds in the enormous double-jointed trucks.

It takes a few minutes to get used to the black night and I am grateful for Pierce's arm as we watch the stars reveal themselves one by one. I would be terrified left alone here tonight; hold that, any night. There's just too much of it all - sky, dark, silence. In the distance, like the lights of a harbour, I can see the few street lamps of Lavit, which comfort me somewhat. To the north-east the campanille of Puygaillard, lit like all the clock towers of France, another point of electric comfort.

Pierce points out the extraordinary breadth of the Milky Way, and crisp star constellations and the air is still warm on our bare arms as we breathe in the sweet scent of unpolluted air. He leaves me still staring in city wonder and returns within seconds with Portia unleashed.

My heart sinks as I watch her slink on to the grass, at first sniffing unsure, then kick-starting her back legs and taking off in a glorious circular gallop, stretching her legs properly for the first time in anywhere other than the concrete car park in the back of the Glasgow flat. Her fur flows and glows in the pale light and amazingly she confines herself to the field's boundaries before returning to sit panting by our side.

'Do you know,' I slur happily. 'I think we'll be fine here.' Taking his eyes briefly from the night sky, Pierce nods in solemn reply. He doesn't know my fingers are crossed behind my back.

I awake the next morning with a thumping head, sun streaming through French doors that are not instantly familiar and Pierce yelling: 'Mum, mum, the men are going now.' In the kitchen every surface is filled with kitchen items but many crates are still untouched. It is only 11.30am.

'Morning,' says Chic. 'We're off now.'

'But you can't leave me like this,' I tell him and his silent helper. 'You're supposed to unpack. That's the deal.'

'Well, you tell us where we can put it, and we will,' he bats back.

He's got me there. I search for my handbag, pull out the envelope with the too-generous tip after wining and dining the buggers, and wave them on their way. Pierce is wonderfully enthusiastic, having slept well, adores the view from his room and despite his own headache, immediately sets to work to get the sitting room straight.

We arrange and re-arrange the furniture, find the sofa covers and the cushions to sit on it, manage even to laugh at the jutting wooden spar that holds an un-shaded lightbulb into the room from the chimney breast. We put up the TV, knowing the Sky men will arrive tomorrow and I find a few of the photographs to put on the gun and card table.

Finally we have a sitting room, sort of. 'Well,' he says, 'It's Lynedoch Street Jim, but not as we know it.' We hear Brian and Paul arrive in tandem – Paul on a scooter, Brian in his car. The smiles are fixed, wary of finding another war scene, but they relax as they see our happy faces.

We go through the house with them asking if x is possible, or if y is possible. The answer of course is always yes, or a better solution is given. Paul moves off to measure walls for the bookcasing and I remember what an exhilarating feeling it is to have money in the bank. Money, I remind myself, which is to be kept as much as possible to generate a bit of interest. They leave to return in a day or two, with the devis - the estimate - which has to be adhered to under French law once we all sign it.

The French gardener, again recommended by Gloria, is the next to turn up. A wiry, wary little chap who walks the fields with me as I lay out a vision of such grandeur even I pause for a moment to think of the cost.

'Above all,' I tell him, 'It's important to keep the grass cut and plant climbers to cover the house and try and make it pretty. Eventually, eventually I'd love little areas in the shade; arbours; paths and oh, some wildflowers. Weeping willows, mulberries, walls....' God, I feel so powerful and in control again.

Back in the house, he accepts a glass of wine, tells me to write out a list of my favourite plants and flowers and he'll come up with a plan. 'Step by step,' he says, 'Little by little.' His accent is the flat Southern sound which adds 'g' to 'n,' puts 'e' instead of 'i', making vin veng and pain peng. I don't know the name of plants in English, never mind French, so in all it's an awfully strange conversation. But fruitful I'm sure, in more ways than one.

When he leaves, promising to return in two days to cut the grass, Pierce says proudly: 'I understood every single thing he said.'

'But you don't speak French,' I reply. 'You gave it up after less than a year.'

'I know,' he says, raising his hands. 'Incredible – I got every word.'

'So why didn't you help me out then?' I say, irritated by his smugness.

'Just because you understand it, doesn't mean you can bloody speak it,' he retorts in the tone used to explain words of more than one syllable. 'Anyway, forget that, where are we going to put the pool?'

Oh yes, the pool. I have £35,000 in the bank account. I had hoped to keep £20,000 of that to generate some interest and have something spare.

Yet, so far, in the space of 24 hours, I have organised estimates for a complete cosmetic make-over never intended of the house; extended the bookcasing from relatively simple shelving to backed, moulded and ventilated furniture; given the gardener a Versailles-style plan of action, which includes full-size instant trees, discussed terracing and making an outdoor sitting/dining room in the mini-stable. The swimming pool, I think, can go on the back-burner for now.

So, in the space of a week, I've acquired a posse of workmen to turn my pig's ear into a silk purse. Sadly they are all Brits – the breed of builders, painters, carpenters and general fixers who are the true colonisers in this new invasion of France.

God knows what some of them did in their old lives. Here they do everything and anything to make a buck and I've relied on the formidable estate agent Gloria to steer me clear of any cowboys.

Most have been here for ten years or more, speak a fluent local dialect overlaid with the unmistakable twang of Manchester, Birmingham or Sarf London. Some are definitely Jack the Lad wide-boys with long baggy shorts and the odd tattoo; stomachs swollen from long lunches and liquid nights, and a swagger of English arrogance as they pace the house in flip-flops.

Others, like my new best friend Paul, produce a meticulous devis for the bookcasing I've asked him to make and painstakingly explains his profit level. I can see why Gloria told me he was a gentleman and came with her full recommendation.

I also know what Paul did in a past life - he was an early roadmanager of the Sex Pistols and is still in touch with them all. Extraordinary.

All, though, are operating on French time, which means 2pm Tuesday is just a point of reference and 4pm Friday is when they actually turn up. Occasionally it is 8pm when they quaff my wine to discuss when they will, maybe, possibly, actually, start work. Work to begin immediately somehow slides into a slot at least a week later, and lunch 'hour' is, of course, noon to 2.30pm.

The gardener has been back twice to discuss when he's coming back to actually start something and he still hasn't produced a devis. Instead, Pierce has mounted the tractor I bought with the house and is making a mean job of knocking the fields into some sort of shape.

At other times he disappears off in the car discovering vales and villages I haven't even seen myself, returning delighted with the beauty around us. French and Sky television is installed and my computer is on the French equivalent of Broadband. It's sobering to realise how desperate this need for contact with the other world is, but vital if I'm to maintain a working life of some kind here.

There is little I can do yet in the unpacking although the kitchen is sorted and we've cleared space on the table to eat. Most nights we go out as it all seems so cheap after Britain and hardly worth the hassle of cooking. I am already craving fish and chips, Chinese and Indian food and wishing for an M&S where I could buy calorie counted microwave meals. This is not a good sign.

Chapter 12

D RIVING back from dropping a bronzed Pierce off at
the airport I try not to focus on my first night alone.
After all I have to get used to it because I've chosen
to live here, confident that I will be fine. God knows why
As I've said, my comfort zone relies on street lighting, the
sound of cars, even dustbin lorries ,in the street, the shouts
of drunks heading home, footsteps on pavements. I like
first-floor living where I can look out at people with a
purpose and know that should I wish to join them, I have
the taxi number on speed dial.

From my Glasgow flat I could turn right and into the city,
or left and into the more diverse West End, taking my pick
of every conceivable ethnic food, meeting friends in bars,
which ranged from wood-panelled snugs to chrome and
glass, minimalist settings.

In 15 minutes I could be at Glasgow Airport heading for
wherever the office chose to send me, knowing that on my
return the bed would be made, the flat cleaned and the dog
returned from her kennels until the next call.

If I chose not to go out at night I could settle content that anything I wanted was there. It's when it's not there that I find one gets restless. And while there is great beauty all around me here, that's basically all there is. That and the silence. I do like country scenes, but usually from behind a plate glass window with a fine-tuned thermostat. I don't necessarily have to be out in it.

Why have I picked something so utterly alien to my needs? Is it the same knee-jerk reaction that brought me here in the first place? Or is it, more likely, the desire to have something so different from what one had rather than a pale imitation of it? After all I could have stayed in Glasgow, traded the flat for a far cheaper one and hacked out a living. But that way there would always have been a hankering back, a looking over the shoulder at what was and a daily realisation of what was lost.

Well, for whatever reason I am here, I've made my bed and there I must lie. The house has that brooding silence that comes when all have departed after a riotous weekend. Even when we're fighting, or Pierce is taking one of his interminable baths, it is comforting to have him here as I turn to sleep. Tonight, alone for the first time, I hear the noises of the day's heat evaporating from the roof tiles, the settling of floor-boards, the ticks and flicks of domestic machinery, all not quite drowned out by the too loud television.

Finally I have to move and go to bed, clipping the lead on Portia for her last outing. Without Pierce I am not confident of just letting her off. I recoil as I step out into the blackness, heart thumping, but stand still waiting for my eyes to become accustomed to the dark. The trees come into vision and the lights of Lavit give me a marker. Bats swoop behind me as I force myself to stay calm and not see imaginary shadows and remind myself to breathe. Portia makes no sound, which is good and is happy to return after doing what she had to do.

I feel very exposed as I walk through the house turning off lights leaving my bedside light and the bare bulb in the bathroom on. I am wide-awake, although it is approaching 2am. I read until the print blurs and the book tries to fall from my hands. Finally I sleep. It is a pattern I am still repeating.

Over the next few days, life settles into a routine. It's an abnormal routine, but a daily rota of sorts. It mainly consists of waiting for the workmen, feeding the workmen, watering the workmen and praying the workmen will actually sod off home.

The workwoman - Cherry - has so far taken two days, two bottles of wine and several spats with her husband to construct three quarters of the flat-pack wardrobe in my room. There are three more to go, two chests of drawers, three non-designed bookcases and she is meant to be painting the other bookcases now being worked on by her husband, Paul. She makes lots of allusions to her therapist. Oh God.

Cherry had first turned up with all Paul's work-tools in the back of a little white van, which has a mini Arsenal kit swinging in the window. Paul has two loves in his life, Cherry and Arsenal, though both can drive him demented depending on their performance. He'd assured me that she could easily knock up the flat-packs; had done it loads of time. She has white-blonde spikey hair pulled back with a band and is a funky Debbie Harry lookalike with the unlined skin of a woman much younger than she actually is. I am astonished when she tells me she's in her early fifties, a few years older than Paul who is her third, or is it fourth, husband.

Cherry adores Paul, red wine and every possible permutation of New Age doctrines. She is the kind of woman who guesses your star sign - wrongly - within 20 minutes of meeting you and wants to feng shui your house. And she has a nervous vulnerability combined with a passionate pride in her husband's skill, which makes her an endearing if intense mix to deal with.

I have decided to be open about the column I write in the Herald Saturday magazine about my life here; making no secret of what I do so that no-one can ever say I was sneaky and observing them for publication behind their backs. I know there are the odd Scots dotted hereabouts and it is quite possible that friends or relatives may see it and recognise the district. It is always anyway far simpler to tell the truth – it is one's greatest defence.

However, Cherry is the first I ask if she minds and if not, would she like me to change her name and Paul's? I show her some columns I have written and she can see I spare neither myself nor Pierce as he constantly reminds me. I find her response both flattering and warm. Her acceptance is immediate, but I double-check with Paul as I still have an uneasy feeling about it. He too thinks it would be a laugh. So, okay then.

Anyway, this morning Cherry has not arrived to continue her battle in my bedroom and Paul is muttering to himself in the kitchen. It appears he is on the verge of a breakdown as he waits to hear if the sale of his London flat has collapsed or not. After eight years in rented houses they plan to buy and need to sell his old flat to make it possible.

He is not being helped in his on-the-brink state by my walls and floors, which run in entirely different directions, never parallel. He constantly curses the wall or fixes it with the sort of stare that could turn a man to, well, stone.

And he constantly apologises for not being his usual self. 'My tank's running on almost empty, Fidelma,' he tells me, almost hyperventilating after the latest mobile call from the lawyer – calls that are coming every half hour now. 'I'll crack up if this falls through.'

And I'll crack up mate if my bookcases fall through and my crack up will be bigger than your crack up is what I'm actually thinking while composing my face into one of sympathy.

He has now just announced that he has to go back to London for a few days to sort things out and Cherry will be a little late today as she's waiting by the phone for news. A little? It's already noon. I don't think either of them is good in the morning.

Brian meanwhile just gets on with the electrics, brings his own sandwiches, and so far appears to have only one tiny problem. His 17 years in France have made him a rather over-enthusiastic double-kisser. And by day three when he cornered me in the kitchen, arms outstretched and lips puckered, I reined him in. I hadn't even brushed my teeth or had a shower for heaven's sake. Hands to his chest, I said firmly: 'Sorry Brian I can't be doing with this thrice a day. I'm not tactile.'

His face crumpled, the lips deflated and he looked genuinely hurt and rather angry. 'But it's the French way. You'll have to get used to it,' he said, a touch huffily.

Really? 'Brian,' I said as gently as I could, 'You're from

Stoke-on-Trent, no matter how long you've lived here. I think not.'

My autocratic Irish grandmother once came home from a dinner party in a state of profound shock. She'd been seated next to a bank manager (trade) and wondered what the world was coming to. She'd be spinning in her grave now if she knew the electrician was attempting to lick my cheeks six times a bloody day.

Well, the sky is blue, the only clouds, the steam from the twin nuclear reactors ten miles, or three seconds away. I checked the distance with Brian who has just come up the stairs to tell me that a recent survey showed that our reactors would not stand up to an earthquake. I think he's just getting his own back for the kissing ban. He stands and peers over my shoulder as I write my column, which features him.

'Am I getting my 15 minutes of fame?' he asks. 'You most certainly are,' I tell him. He disappears back to his electrics rather pleased with life.

Last night, Jean Pierre, the gardener, turned up at 7.30 for a glass of red and yet another discussion as to when he'd next turn up. He hasn't actually done anything yet, but this is now our fourth meeting to discuss meeting. Thank God Pierce liked playing on the tractor or I'd be hacking through the undergrowth in search of Portia.

I'm to present him with the list of plants, hedges, climbers, trees I like and his daughter will come and draw up a plan. So I spend a happy few hours with my new stack of French gardening books and terms, creating my stunning vista of weeping willows, arbours, winding avenues of lavender, box hedging, cypress tunnels.

However, on closer look it is plain that I've gone a stage beyond even Versailles and a probable bill to match.

After Jean Pierre left I realised it was the first time in days I had spent more than an hour speaking French. With English workers, Sky TV and e-mailing, it is actually possible to live in a little bubble of Britishness. Indeed many do. One woman I met, and am now desperately avoiding, has lived here for 15 years. I said: 'Your French must be amazing.'

'Oh no,' she answered. 'I'm not interested in doing that. You don't need to.'

Even the supermarkets have shelves dedicated to HP sauce, baked beans, and oddly, piccalilli. It's only walking out into the scorching heat that it hits me that I really am in the South of France.

I need to get out more. I need to sign up to the cultural club in Lavit and get my dance card marked by a few neighbouring farmers. Or book up for one of the numerous village soirées celebrating every variety of Saint. Lotto is very big around here too, which would help my number block, but I'm not sure I could cope with the prizes which seem to be live - like hens, ducks or even goats. I cannot believe I am seriously contemplating going to bingo.

But I'll need to find my clothes first and a pair of heels. And for that I need a wardrobe. There is still no sign of Cherry. In her other life she is a heavy-metal sculptress, trained in London and Paris, but wasps have colonised her studio and she can't work, which makes her very manic, she admits.

Unfortunately not manic enough to blitz the Ikea packs. Maybe I should steal her medication. Yesterday she upped tools at 4.30pm and downed them at 6.30pm, disappointed she said that she wasn't further along. She looked so miserable, shoulders sagging, staring at the fruits of her labour that I didn't have the heart to suggest why. And I couldn't quiz her on the marks gouged into the doors by her dodgy use of the power tools. 'Design fault,' she mouthed, following my eyes.

I have got into a bad habit of offering 'one for the road,' and Cherry shows no inclination of refusing; nor me of joyfully joining her. Is it because I don't have a real life here yet, or is it because drinking wine at every opportunity is what you think you should do in France? Maybe it's because we're able to sit outside in light and warmth, wearing shorts and t-shirts. Again, that permanent holiday feeling.

Paul - who accepts a bottle of beer - and herself start to bicker again over the timings for his plane to London and who has organised what and where. Portia gives me a warning look and heads for the sofa.

All I care about is not missing Eastenders and trying to get an answer as to when they might return and I can get my clothes out of the removal wardrobes. I suggest they wait and have their domestic at home and a bit shame-faced, Paul tells her to swig up.

I'm growing very fond of them, but enough is enough. Left finally to myself, I have an orgy of oven chips, two fried eggs, lashings of malt vinegar and switch on Eastenders, eating on a tray in front of the television. When I finish I accept I am obviously going downhill fast.

So? One can't eat foie gras all the time. And anyway wardrobe-less women need every bit of comfort they can get is what I tell Portia who has raised her head to give me the look of shame.

Next morning with no workmen, being a Saturday, I decide to go off to market. Well, no workmen except Cherry who astonishes me by turning up at 10am to continue her assault on the wardrobe. I don't know who is more shocked by her appearance – her or me.

'Well with Paul going to London we thought we'd come here today instead,' she says clutching her breakfast baguette and heading for where I keep the coffee. 'He'll be along soon. Where you going then?'

'To market,' I say in the new sing-song voice I've adopted here and an attitude that suggests it is a normal thing for me.

'Oh, right,' she says absent-mindedly walloping my butter on her bread, stuffing it with my ham. 'Honest?' Thought you didn't cook?'

Well, no, I don't, but apparently this is what one is meant to do in France. I've read the books and all the salivating prose about sniffing the goats' cheese, goosing the melons, prodding the tomatoes. I can be that woman. Fortunately, the last owners left a large rattan basket behind, so I can look the part at least. I leave her to it.

Using the tank as a battering ram in the French way, I find a parking space close to the square, adjust my sunglasses and flip-flop onwards as purposively as any French housewife. Moissac's week-end market is one of the finest in the south west. In the open air the stalls overflow with fruit, vegetables, honey, plants, spices; jostling for space with bag and pottery sellers, clothes racks and the massive truck which opens up to reveal scores of hideous shoes.

Here the melon seller asks when it is intended to be eaten and when told, searches, feels and smells before handing you perfection. Even though I am deeply impressed, I make the sort of face that shows it is just what I expect.

Inside les halles, fish and seafood glisten on trays of ice a few steps away from the horse butcher who bizarrely displays photographs of horses playing in sun-dappled fields. It's strange isn't it that we can look at pictures of cows with the cuts picked out in dotted curves and squares and don't even flinch? But horses? Dear oh dear.

It is only the British who stand aghast, eyes flicking from picture to fillet and back again, painful memories of my little pony etched on the women's faces; memories of fat little Cinders who carried them safely over the two-foot high jumps. Memories of times when ecstasy was an afternoon spent asleep on urine-sodden straw next to an over-kissed, snuffling, at times evil, little beast.

First love with all the pain of a vicious nip in the upper arm when putting the bit into a reluctant mouth. First love recalled when seeing fat little Cinders' twin, now pictured above the dark red meat that she became after a quick trip to the killing shed.

Being a local now, I am made of sterner stuff and shuffle by, eyes down, to the cheese counter. I have my first guests this week-end and I aim to dazzle with a table brimming over with genuine French fare and flair. I have to dazzle because Jacqui and Gordon are driving from the famous Colombe d'Or in Saint Paul de Vence, where their fellow guests this week include Rod Stewart, Roger Moore and Nigel Havers.

Here they have Pierce's mattress, a lamp and un-ironed

sheets because I haven't found the iron yet. They do have their own bathroom and I have cleared a track around the table and found some candlesticks. I am still searching for the candles. Jacqui can also catch up on the omnibus editions of Corrie and Eastenders, which she has missed while luxuriating in the far south.

Meanwhile, back at Las Molières, bless her, Cherry is still wrestling with the wardrobe, day four. I'll discover she has already ditched two baskets and two drawers in a bid to get the doors on, muttering that it must be a design fault. Definitely a design fault. Why am I not surprised?

As I have never been a dazzler at the table, faced with a multitude of cheeses, I freeze. There are goats' cheeses done up to look like tarts with apricots and strawberries pressed into their rounds; hunks for melting over potatoes; dried out looking yellowy chunks, which the locals are buying en masse and thankfully, the old familiar Brie and Camembert. Confused, I think I'll just buy a bit of everything. As I drop them into the basket - man, I feel like a woman.

On to the oysters, the langoustines and the fish. I realise that with none of my cookery books unpacked I'm stymied. I wouldn't know where to start, and I couldn't start anyway without a recipe telling me everything I needed to go with the fish or the seafood and what to do with it.

If I tell you that I once heard Pierce reply to a little pal's question of 'what does your mother make for dinner?' with the damning: 'a reservation;' you'll get the picture. But I look with the harsh eye of an expert on what is laid before me and think 'merde,' knowing I haven't a clue what to do with any of it. I have the uneasy feeling that France is showing me up for the incapable soul I am.

I flip-flop on to the meat counter. Breasts of duck would be classic. No cookery book. Lamb chops? Too boring. All the other meat? You're joking. My inadequacies are overwhelming me and I'm aware of other Anglos smelling and pressing this bit and that bit and discussing with 'darling' whether they should grill, marinade or ceviche the choice cuts. Using clipped, almost deliberately English accented French to quiz the fishmonger, the butcher and the vegetable grower on their products before pointing to what they will take.

Without even hearing them, you know they're Brits. It's the shape of the women, particularly from the back. The bleached chinos, or the cut-off linen trousers with a narrow little belt over the pear outline of the backside. The neat little hair-cut and across-the-body purse. The au-naturel nails, beaten into squared and buffed submission and the un-made up faces loaded with factor 1005 under a childish fringe.

The husbands aren't much better. Long shorts crisped to just above the knee, the occasional varicose vein pumping blood behind a meaty knee, the voluptuous stomach rippling over the waistband. The polo player on their rather daring pink or lime green short-sleeved shirt. Their bulging, greedy faces as they try wine, swilling it around their gerbil cheeks, and their grudging delight or slight disgust in the resultant swallow. For God's sake just buy it I want to scream in my newly found Frenchness.

May God forgive me for all these nasty observations. Who am I to judge, peering myopically into their middle-class idyll, feeling so above it all with my jaundiced eyes and new found pride as a resident? I live here. Not like these gîte dwelling Southerners. Oh shit, maybe they do live here and these will be my new best friends.

Actually if I'm being really honest, I'm a little envious of such couples. I know these women can knock up meals for ten out of what they keep in their store cupboard and greet their children with kisses and 'darlings' instead of hitting them over the head with Michelin Map books. Yes, I'm jealous of their pear-shaped English bums and their controlled lives attended on by men who are called Tim and Anthony. The feeling doesn't last though as I watch them trudge off together in the weary, isolated silence of too much knowledge of each other.

Well, at least I can buy stuff for a salad - I've a bottle of ready-made dressing. (Can't do that either without a cookery book.) This is real lettuce. Loads of different ones, even different colours, which I'll have to strip and wash peering into the folds in case of slugs. None of your ready-washed M&S continental mixed bags here. Sigh.

However, my bag is taking on a comfortable, ethnic bulge. Stallholders smile warmly at me - they know a woman who instinctively knows what to do with a pile of raw food. Well with a melon, a salad and some cheese. This is not enough.

But I already know that all is not lost because I've wandered here before when house searching. One corner of les halles is taken up with a wondrous sight. Dressed in chef's whites, a smiling man and several women churn out... ready-made meals. Using gigantic pans they make an incredible paella, shovelling into the rice, mussels, langoustines, chicken wings and handfuls of saffron and paprika. The smell is out of this world. So is the smell coming from the other enormous pan. Sauté potatoes mixed with onions and garlic, fried just short of peak, ready for a last few minutes in the pan.

I order large plastic take-aways of both; fling in two free-range chickens and a ham from the rotisserie for good measure and stagger with my basket to the wine counter.

Now I know what I'm talking about. For less than three quid a bottle I buy four vintage Bouzet, from the local château, three rosés from the nearby Gaillac and have a little taster of each. The five-litre boxes are already stacked in the kitchen.

I now have to practically drag my rattan bag from market. The sweat is running down me; the hair plastered to my face and I am no longer a chic shopper. Just an old bag-woman with her cairry-oot.

Twenty minutes later, re-hydrated by the tank's air-conditioning I arrive back at Las Molières. All is quiet. Too quiet. In the bedroom Cherry and Paul are staring at the wardrobe. I notice another basket has been ditched. Paul has his baseball cap on backwards and is regarding Cherry with the exasperated expression of a man who has been trying to explain something whilst retaining his temper. I look at the basket and back at Cherry.

'Definitely a design fault,' she says. 'There's nowhere for half these things to go.'

'But they were designed in the shop, on the computer, to fit,' I throw back as a question really.

'I know,' she says scratching her head. 'They've got it wrong.'

'Could you have got it wrong?' I suggest more than question, giving her the opening.

'Nah.'

Well that's that then.

Paul leaves tonight for London and the first bookcase is only half finished and now he has to sort the wardrobe. Cherry also points out two marks on the doors. They look like the marks made when a screwdriver has slipped and dug into the casing. We peer at them for some time. 'See, another design fault,' she finally comes up with.

It's time to get tough. I will not be messed about with. 'Red or white?' I ask, with a look that warns don't ask for rosé.

Chapter 13

GOD I'm gorgeous! Each morning I wake up here and stagger to the bathroom and peer at my nut-brown self. No matter how many vins rouge taken the night before, to overcome the fear of the night, I still look incredibly healthy.

My hair is bleached blonde; the facial lines are bronzed not grey and the usual pallid bit between neck and cleavage is chestnut. It's amazing, especially considering that France is having its worst summer in years and we can go from 40 degrees to 20 degrees in 24 hours. C'est pas normale, say the locals when I ask if I've arrived in France as it has turned into Scotland thanks to global warming.

I do keep searching for signs of yellow on my skin, i.e. liver failure, because, without a doubt I have become the mad (well madder) old lush my son warned me I'd become. It's nothing to do with the fact that wine, good wine, is so cheap here, but all to do with that feeling of being on permanent holiday.

And on holiday you crack open the wine. I've avoided

bottles because this is a recyclable country and I really can't be bothered with all that – so I'm into the five-litre boxes. Unfortunately, it is hard to monitor one's intake when pressing the little red button… again and again and again.

In all seriousness, the drink is a problem here and not just with the Brits who seem to have a genetic predisposition to fall easily into happy valley waiting for the clock to strike 1pm for the first of the day. I'm learning that, although one never, ever, sees the French drunk in public, there is a 'behind closed doors' major issue. Here in rural France it was common for the men to have consumed a litre before lunch plus cognac for breakfast. But the French road traffic death toll and a new punitive purge by the police have changed all that.

In the village bar, there are still the drinkers in by 11am - now with a few women. But in the main it is a private thing. A dark art practised away from prying eyes. I hear whispers of men who drink steadfastly and bitterly and raise their fists to their wives. The wives who appear in public with bruises and dark circles under the eyes caused by sleepless wariness as to what may come.

Backwater France is still a land where women are considered by many to be still inferior in society but very important in the home. Their life is, and according to their men, should be, devoted to their families.

A woman like me has to be careful not to be the red-rag to the bull. So, I would never go down to the pub of an evening and chat. That could make me louche, easy, a bit of a girl. I can go before lunch and maybe have an aperitif, just one, with the dog, to watch the world go by - but nothing more.

Women here, apart from a few tough ones, do not drink with the men and have a laugh and a chat. I've never been a stand-at-the-bar woman anyway, so it isn't something I'm missing. But the bar is the place to hear who's the good workman, who's the one to be avoided and to find help and advice.

But I'm also aware that to quietly sip one drink and make light conversation also makes me a little suspect. It is back to nuances again. In English one can make plain by words and gestures that you are simply in a place for a drink and a moment in time. In France, desperate to communicate you can often come across as simply... well, desperate. It is a tricky situation and one I'm grappling with.

I had hoped, that by virtue of age, no one would see me as a threat. But sadly, there are quite a few English women 'of a certain age' who have come to this region and have made it clear that they are available. And they have been taken up. I have heard the stories and I cringe at what these women are doing. But then it is not for me to judge. Loneliness can make fools of us all.

Somehow I think my dead-eye stare makes it clear that I am not available. I hope so.

But it doesn't stop me coming home and pouring another glass. I do it to dull the coming night because I am still scared of the dark and my place in this land. I use the wine to curb my fears and get me to bed and hope that once everything is perfect around me, I won't need to.

Which is rubbish. Even in long-gone five-star hotels, I left the light on in the bathroom and had another glass of wine. Isn't it ridiculous? To be in one's 50s and still scared of the dark. To have a house in the French countryside and be afraid of nature, be afraid of everything? Still, better to be on the road to mad lushdom than picking up French farmers in bars.

I can ponder all this in the awesome silence of the house. The Blessed Brian, who arrives on the dot at 9.30 every morning, works steadily away and leaves at 6.30pm, is having a rare day off.

Paul's tools and benches lie unused in the kitchen. He has a problem with mornings, so I didn't worry too much until lunchtime. His trip to London had been partially successful and he was awaiting word that the money was in the bank all last week and there were flashes of the cheeky chappie he promised I'd see.

I phone their house and leave a message. An hour later Cherry phones me whispering. He is having a breakdown, apparently. Lying on the sofa, unable to talk or move. Something about the house sale. She's never seen him like this. She thinks she's about to have one too because we're close to a full moon. I haven't a clue if the painter they've chosen is also having one as there's no sign of him on his supposed first day. No, says Cherry earnestly, he's okay, but because of their breakdowns there's no one able to drive him here. A fair enough explanation.

What is the etiquette in asking how long they think their crack-ups will last? I tell them to both get better soon and phone me as soon as they're able to work again. As I'm living in the same handful of clothes anyway, who needs a wardrobe? I've got a carefully planned rat-run around all the boxes and a clear view of the telly.

I head for the rosé in the box, ping a glassful, grab a book and go lie in the sun to top up my gorgeousness. After an hour during which I become acutely aware of the rapidly growing grass I decide I'll give Jean Pierre a call to organise another meeting to discuss his arrival to actually do something. I'm stunned when he answers; even more so when he promises he will be here the day after tomorrow, Monday. 'With the machines that will cut the grass?' I ask in my usual convoluted way. There is a little laugh. 'Little by little. Step by step.'

I decide I have a philosopher gardener. Which is good. But I may also have a gardener who never actually gardens. Which is not so good. Well at least he's not in the throes of a breakdown.

Come the morning I decide to put Portia in the tank and head for St Nick and a walk around the plan d'eau, where the Tarn and Garonne rivers meet in confluence in a carved out lake made possible by the profits of the nuclear industry. It is indeed a glorious leisure spot with open-air swimming club, yacht and boat hire and meandering walks beside which campers are welcome. The grounds leading to the water are groomed by young boys in an almost Disney World ritual of perfection. Irrigation sprays keep the grass swards green and crisp.

Often I meet maybe two, three other souls. Runners from nearby Moissac pacing themselves around the lake with its discreet information boards of which birds migrate here to breed. Or office workers having a picnic lunch, ties off, shirt open, mini wine bottle giving them just one glass to accompany an often incredible array of food from plastic containers. I never cease to be amazed at the number of such high-maintenance public pleasure spaces in this country and how underused, in our terms, they are.

We aren't long out of Lavit when I see her. She is walking

towards us up the dusty road, an old handbag firmly clasped against her navy blue belted dress, wearing half-gloves of lace to cover her hard-working hands, no doubt swollen and twisted, perhaps slightly arthritic.

On her bunned grey hair is a dark blue Panama hat and one knew instinctively that this is a woman walking to 11am Mass, in Lavit. It means, by my rough calculation, that she still has a mile and a half to go and Lord knows how far she's already walked on her road to salvation.

She stops in her stride to return my wave, half-raising her arm, half-smiling, before she knows she hasn't a clue who I am, and reverts to the piercing, rather sullen stare of the French paysanne. I do not insult her by that word. I only mean to ground her in her place, in her land, in her history. She would use it herself. It is only us who have twisted such words into sneering put-downs.

I watch her in the rear mirror as she watches me, before, with a slight shrug, she steps off again in the sultry heat. On her feet are navy leather court shoes; her legs are encased in nylon, probably pop socks stretched up and over her knees, way, way above the dress swishing against her calves.

She must be 80 at least, and once, in her youth, she'd have pulled on her sheer stockings, securing them with elastic garters which would have made permanent indents in her thighs. For some reason it makes me smile to think of her pulling up her pop socks every morning, after years of suffering the tourniquet of the garter. What a blessed release.

I don't think to stop and offer her a lift back towards the squat church where St John Vianney - his statue at least -

lurks darkly inside the doorway. I doubt she would accept one, or at least that's how I'll rationalise it later. This is what she does and I am but a blip, an almost nothing in her normality.

Anyway as I watch her retreating march in the rear view suddenly, in spite of the fields of corn and sunflowers, the way-side walnut trees and a cloudless sky, I am back in my Irish childhood.

Madame could be a County Kilkenny farmer's wife heading into town and the Black Abbey - a walk of three miles and back, an easy stroll, a 'stretch of the legs, girl,' and a time to ponder on the sins she believes besmirch her soul.

It's her time of preparation, contemplation – a walk in tune with a rhythmic rendition of 'Holy Marys' and 'Our Fathers,' with the odd 'Glory be' thrown in. If she passed a cemetery there would be several 'eternal rests' mouthed for her own family, all named of course, the friends long gone, all named of course, the souls with no-one left to pray for them, and finally, for all the souls in purgatory who need every prayer to nudge them further up the ladder to eternal light.

I hope no one ever tells her that the present Pope has decreed Purgatory is no more. We all need a half-way house between heaven and hell, and someone to pray for us.

So, I recognise, and somehow hear all this, within the space of seeing her and passing her, as her arm reached up to return my wave. I know of this woman and her life so far from mine. I know her thoughts; her yearnings. I can sense, feel, the inner melody, which matches her heavy footprints, carries her along the road all the women have trod before her. I know of her prayers.

For even now, dressed in my Prada chinos, my feet in Tod loafers, my nails painted in Chanel rouge noir; my hair high and low-lighted, sitting on the leather seats of my turbo pumped 4X4, I drive, if not walk, to exactly the same rhythm, reciting the same litany of prayers.

Like her (of this I'm sure) I cannot sleep without the rituals, ending with 'there are four corners to my bed, there are four angels around my head. Matthew, Mark, Luke and John, bless the bed that I lie on.'

And I know, in her own language, she also intones the mantra: 'If I should die while I'm awake, I pray to God my soul to take. If I should die while I'm asleep, I pray to God my soul to keep.' And finally, like me, I know she'll say a perfect act of contrition before being at last able to close her eyes.

To say the words is to weave a canopy of protection around our bed. Hers, no doubt a high dark oak, unsprung platform redolent of sacrifice and stoicism; mine a self-indulgent mix of goose down and suede panels, soft linen and fake-fur throw.

Yet, for all our differences in age, nationality and lifestyle, like her, I cannot pass a cemetery without the incantations and all the names, always adding others, (including a special category for all the journalists who drank their way to the grave.) It is an exhausting journey as one fumbles for name after name, superstitiously aware that to miss one means to start all over again.

I know all this in my Irish soul, my English, ambitious, feminist heart, and in whatever I have ultimately become.

A hack who would still sell out such a woman if she had a story I needed. But, for the moment I only know there is something in her which touches me out of my permanent abstract state of observance and throws me back to another time.

Since coming here, I've had many such time-flips of familiarity. Sudden lurches into the past; waves of something lost which are scrabbling at the edges of my brain, nibbling at a mind daily losing memories of yesteryear - a mind which sometimes can't recall a conversation of a week ago. Yet seeing this old woman on a French country road instantly releases a flood of longing and a torrent of mental images.

I feel increasingly in this part of France a sense of returning to the 50s and a way of life long lost to us. It is the cliché we all seem to use who have ended up here living another cliché, 'living the dream,' or in truth for most, nowhere else to run to.

Here old women dress with formality and dignity, and there is a relinquishing of all attempts at sexuality and yes, by definition faux-fertility. There are no attempts to hold back, or shun, time and squeeze their sagging bodies into elasticated jeans and T-shirts emphasising breasts, which are elongated and empty. No make-up employed to tease the lips into baby pouts, grotesque parodies of what they once were.

By day old fashioned pinnies, tied in a thin bow at the sides, cover weighty bosoms; hair, its natural grey, is clasped back into buns or pulled high on the head, and the conker-brown faces of these women, heavily lined by the sun, tell of a lifetime of hard work and pain - with the same hint of resignation just about still evident in our women.

But there is also a sort of detached, almost slightly contemptuous, contentment.

The men are the same, minus the pinnies and the buns, although they do not have the knowing butterfly layers which shimmy over the eyes of the females, assessing, grading, sifting all in front of them - plopping out the grit; rubbing away the irritants which pollute their lives.

Men rarely do, it seems, in any corner of the world. But, again, like the Irish countrymen I once observed, they play their part, liking nothing better than to sit on the side of the road watching the world go by.

Every morning three old boys gather to sit on a bench at the roundabout out of Lavit. Should it lightly rain they move as one to a window ledge on the other side of the road. Of indeterminate age, hair covered by cap or beret, they sit in comfortable silence watching the infrequent passing traffic, saluting those they know, blatantly staring, like the women, at those they don't. So far they haven't returned my waves, squaring their jaws in case a twitch gives me hope. I haven't earned a response yet.

In neighbouring St Nicolas, the boules court off the main square is filled with old men bowling or watching - hurling insults at each other with the ease of those whose friendship began in childhood and who have neither questioned nor sought a different way of life.

Men like my neighbour, Monsieur Dupont whose sprawling farm lies four fields and two roads from me, linking land with his son's, no doubt edging that of his cousins.

Small, like all the local men, and exuding a fizzing energy and musty body heat, he could be anywhere between 60 and 75. I notice some teeth are missing, others stained and twisted.

He has the gestures and thick, thick accent of all around here - ending his words with a gutteral g, turning a's into e's, and answering 'oc' instead of 'oui' for yes. The lines and creases on his face and neck are the deep, deep brown of an outdoors man in a hot climate, almost black at the nape of the neck. Yet there is a grave attractiveness about him - a knowing innocence.

He'd arrived in the small two-seater white van used by every farmer and artisan in the area. Having just two seats takes it into a category which allows the VAT to be reclaimed when it needs garage attention. A small saving, but an important one to the French. We shake hands having met when I searched for Portia who'd raced through his fields when Paul started using his nail gun.

He is entranced by the Afghan, her beauty and speed transcending his entrenched beliefs that dogs are for working or hunting. I suspect he's relieved that, when I say they are hunting dogs, he can believe that he has not gone suddenly soft. I do not add that her line has been long bred for the length and silk of her coat and the hunter's intelligence has been lost in the mix.

Monsieur Dupont asks if I have bought Las Molières as a holiday home. I answer, to his apparent pleasure that I will be living here permanently. However, he affects a look of baffled inquiry as I praise the beauty of the countryside around us. With a shrug he says he never notices it – he has lived where he was born all his life. But his eyes shift and gleam and I know he has a passionate love and pride in this land. Not that he would ever use such words.

Jean Pierre, the gardener, is the same, living within two miles of where he was born, feigning nonchalance at the wonders around him as if he too has never noticed his surroundings. It would be both insulting and wrong to these men and women to romanticise them as simple people close to the soil, honed by hard toil and in the past, poverty.

Their lives will have been, and are, as complex and troubled as any urban dweller. In their midst are also the sly, the cunning, the malcontents, the idlers, the ones who can see no good in others, or even any worth, or splendour in the fields and nature around them. Their history is too brutal, and their lands too often ravaged by war and natural phenomena, to have created benign generations.

But there is no doubt their ease and apparent contentment with their lot comes from the land, from knowing their place - in the true sense of the phrase. Knowing every inch of field and ditch and every boundary within the forests. Translating the undulations of the clouds, aware of the sudden quick wind which arrives seconds before a darkening sky and precedes a storm, or deceptively moves away quickly, twisting to rain-lash a more vulnerable crop.

The French have an expression about women of a certain age who have a serene beauty. It roughly translates as being 'well in her skin.' Again, it is rooted in contentment. Acceptance, not resignation, of what she is and what she has and what she has been. The beauty is not necessarily a physical beauty. It can be in the bearing of a fat, untidy old woman; in the haughty carriage of middle-aged matrons pushing a trolley around 'Leclerc.'

It is though, always found in the eyes. A calmness, a

steady gaze that never flicks over a shoulder for something or someone more interesting. And it is what I'm increasingly aware of in the eyes of the old men and women around me.

It is not in the eyes of the young. Their eyes are already fixed on the cities, on the life available through television and the internet, and their gaze lingers distastefully, if anything, on the land whose tranquillity is a reminder of all they're missing. Their disaffection shows in their restless twilight walks around Lavit; little groups of girls and boys killing time until the pizza is ready for 'emporter.'

It shows in their ceaseless texting on their latest mobile phones, their desultory prowl around the steel posts of the village halle, scuffing their feet as if exhausted by the boredom of it all. It shows in the dispirited way they pick at the pizzas, not really hungry, just desperate to get away from the closed shutters of the stone houses keeping them fast from possible adventures.

In some ways they are no different from the teenagers in the rural and suburban areas of the UK, desperate to find a different life. But their very innocent outbreaks of pizza hunger and walkabouts are a world away from our drink-sodden offspring waiting to pick fights with a father remonstrating against their noise and foul language.

These 'children,' for here they still are, despite their cut-offs and ripped T-shirts, say 'bonjour' on entering a shop; pause to allow their elders to leave first and whisper quietly into their mobiles when waiting in the porch of the restaurant for those pizzas.

But their yearning for city life is why people like me now have those farmhouses and cottages to buy as farming communities dwindle and cities swell to unheard-of French proportions. It's why Monsieur Dupont relates sadly that he no longer knows the people who have taken over many of the houses, once home to several generations of families.

To him they are just a blur of UK number plates speeding past him on his road. They arrive, spill out, stretch out beside the newly dug pools, hold parties from which the music travels over the fields late at night, then disappear, leaving their barred, locked and shuttered houses to sit deserted until the following summer.

Even his own people are often a mystery to him now. He shrugs with an eloquence borne of experience about the young who may never know what it is to be content and accept what one has. They are the ones who have left, will leave, and have allowed us in. At least the houses live on.

The irony of course, is that we arrive from our towns and cities, faces filled with similar discontent, spoilt and pampered, used to instant gratification yet yearning to be well in our skin. Seeking roots, perhaps, after a lifetime avoiding them.

It is easy to spot us as we walk aimlessly around the squares and alleys. It is not the hire-cars we've arrived in, nor the British number plates on our own. Not the clutch of estate agents' magazines in our hand nor the scanning of their windows. It's not even the pale skin and the particular set of features that instantly define us all under one group – les Anglo Saxons.

No, it's the twist to the mouth, the quickening from mild interest to disappointment as a glance around the village makes us annoyed that it has failed to live up to the fantasy. It's the sulky pursed lips of failure when the anticipation has outweighed the reality. The irritability when the café has closed, the chambres d'hôtes is full, the immobilier shut, when the sign says clearly it should be open.

But it's also that yearning, that flicker of hope and that inward prayer to be well in our skin and seek out the roots we've avoided for so, so long. A vulnerability somehow that marks us out from the Dutch and the Belgians who also follow the path to here.

Perhaps, that's why I see and feel an Ireland long gone too, everywhere I look. An Ireland no longer quite there when I go back; somehow tantalisingly out of reach, but only just. One I'm certain is just around the next country lane. One where I'll chance again upon myself, singing as I skip between the lupin hedgerows, hurrying to feed an impatient pony.

It's here though, in every roadside shrine. In every statue of Our Lady, arms reaching out in the courtyard of a silent village school; in the bunches of fresh wild flowers laid under a glassed-in roadside crucifix miles from anywhere.

I hear it in the church bells that ring out the Angelus at noon and again at six, and if the men in the fields no longer stop for prayers and the tractors keep on ploughing, it still seems as if they have. It still feels as if someone, somewhere is quietly crossing himself and reflecting on a spiritual need.

I feel it in the surge of a surprising emotion when I chance upon an old woman in a blue dress walking steadfastly to Mass, her weathered and worn good leather handbag firmly pressed under her arm. I smell it walking past the meadows of wildflowers and grasses - hear it in the busy /

indolent hum of bees and the buzz attack of insects a backdrop to the intensity of the perfumes in an otherwise silent as a stone countryside.

And it's there in the urgent falls of the weirs in the rivers that flow through so many towns, seen from ancient bridges, electric light hidden behind curled iron carriage lamps. Long, long forgotten memories rush back to me, sharper than anything this last year. Sharper even than the misery of my arrival where my loneliness shocked and depressed me, plunging me to depths of despair.

And for the first time I realise it is not a future I'm seeking here. It's the past.

Chapter 14

IT seemed innocent enough. A plain white envelope in my mail box, locally posted. Inside there was a printed letter headed 'Welcome to the Paper-book Swap' and instructions to send a used paperback to the first name on an enclosed list of two, then remove name one, move name two to one and put your name as No 2. Then send copy of the new list to six of your friends and basically in the end, 36 used paperbacks will wing their way here.

It has been sent to me by a woman who added a handwritten note saying: 'Hope you don't mind – I know we haven't met but I'm new here too and got to five, not six.'

Am I being churlish and sour when I say actually I do mind? I have enough used paperbacks to supply the whole of the Tarn et Garonne for a year and a pathological dislike of chain letters, even worthy ones.

But, and here's the dilemma, this is a missive from the heart of the Brit community, members of which, I'm rather disconcerted to discover, are dotted all over the hills and vales in far greater numbers than I realised. I'm discovering them because slowly, but surely they're finding me whether by unnanounced arrival or out-of-the blue telephone call.

Others have phoned to say a friend of a friend said I might be interested in meeting them. Some I have met when they loudly take over La Florentin, in Moissac after the Sunday market, legs sprawling across the pavement in arrogant possession, braying their nationality while running far from their nation.

Barring a few exceptions, I am uneasy in their company as they happily admit that even after, in some cases, 20 years of living in France, they neither speak the language nor have any French friends. Few have been over the doors of their neighbouring farmers' houses nor thought of inviting their neighbours for the ritual aperitif.

Some basically tell me that they love France despite the French, and others begin conversations with a condescending: 'The people here are really lovely, helpful but...' One woman actually said: 'They don't like it when you speak English to them you know. They can be quite uppity.'

What planet are these people on? She couldn't grasp what I was saying when I'm afraid, rather coldly I replied: 'You've just spent an hour ranting on about how horrific it is with what's happening in Britain with all the immigrants. So presumably you'd back a Pole or Romanian's right to speak Polish and Romanian and not learn English? And if they suggested that you should learn their language you'd probably be a bit miffed, wouldn't you?'

Her friends around the table stiffened, unused to being

challenged, particularly by a newcomer. 'It's hardly the same though, is it?' she sniffed.

Excuse me madame, it is exactly the same. I backed off a little then, having already mentally ticked them off my possibles list, for despite not really caring for their good opinion, I still don't want to end up as Norma No-Mates. It could be a long hard winter here and some of these may be the best I can hope for. It's a desperate thought.

At times recently I've felt I'm in a colonial vacuum, with a disturbing undercurrent of right-wing prejudice and a pride in non-political correctness bordering on a reckless racism. I too, eschew the barmier aspects of our new pc Britain, but there have always been core values, morals and behaviour, which decent people adhere to. Here I've heard words directed towards Britain's immigrants, which have shocked me rigid.

I think of my eclectic mix of friends and acquaintances in Glasgow and London and understand as never before that like goes to like. I'd heard these people existed, but I never thought I might break bread with them. I have become a true snob in my distaste. My look of disgust I hope has branded me unsuitable for further invitations.

Paul the cabinet maker calls them the wine-louts and mimics the weekly scenes at Toulouse Airport; the men in their Panamas shouting to friends coming off the easyJet Gatwick hell: 'Henry – marvellous to see you old boy. Got a superb Bordeaux awaiting your pleasure.'

Back to his cheery chappie self, thank God, with his sale problems sorted, he has me in tears with his parody as he struts around the kitchen, shoulders back to support the weight of their enormous stomachs, my Panama hat over his shaved head, the grin of false bonhomie perfectly etched on his features.

He also knows they mimic him and his Eastenders accent and wonder how the hell he was allowed in to their paradise. And then he mimics them mimicking him, splaying his feet in his flip-flops, pulling his reverse baseball cap further down to his eyebrows, scratching his armpit in exaggerated pleasure.

But it's the Pauls and the Brians and many of the other chippies, handymen and electricians, who are truly experiencing French life. They play in the village football teams; their children go to school becoming fluent in no time; they sit table to table alongside their French neighbours at the chasse dinners and the fête paella nights. They learn of the fights and the feuds and are greeted by those glowering French grandmothers with kisses and smiles as one of their own.

Without benefit of private or further education they shame the others, quickly speaking a rapid local patois, joshing with the ease and familiarity of their hard-won acceptance. It doesn't matter that their accents are often atrocious and their grammar non-existent and that the swagger, the baseball hats and baggy shorts scream Brit builder – they have grabbed their new life and will do everything to preserve and enjoy it. They are accepted - working hard and long, prepared to turn their hands to anything to give them the means to live here, and the vast majority are registered, paying tax and often heavy social charges.

Their presence has saved many a village from dying yet they are looked down on by jumped-up retired middle-managers who sold a semi in Suburbiton to buy a maison de campagne in France, re-inventing themselves along the way into a Noël Coward version of the Englishman abroad. Who can't even stir themselves to learn the language.

And it's true that here they have a greater chance of mixing in company they only aspired to in the past. I shock them with my questions and my openness that I'm here because I needed somewhere cheap to live. Pierce's father told me long ago that I ask the questions at dinner parties that other people want to ask, but wouldn't dream of doing so in a million years. I had a vague grasp of what he meant so now I ask the questions by first adding the rider: 'Forgive me if this is rude, but in my job it's normal... do you, did you, what made you, where were you, etc. etc.' Often they're so shocked they answer and I flatter myself that the night is made richer for it.

It's only the ones who have something to conceal; the ones playing a new role who look back at me with an almost apoplectic rage. Perverse as I may be, I love that moment because I know I've hit the Achilles' heel, which is what made me good at my job but also, obviously at times pretty obnoxious.

Also so many of these people have too much time on their hands, fixed incomes, retirement pensions and a lingering attachment to a way of life unaffordable to them in Britain now. Oh did I just describe myself? For my sanity I refuse to think that way. I cashed in the pensions early, I'm still working, ten to 15 years younger than all of them - and - the day I take up line-dancing or water-colours, I will take myself to the library with the gun and do the decent thing.

After yet another drinks party on an enviable terrace, I come home to wonder what the hell I'm getting myself into. It seems, and I say this tentatively as a raw newcomer, that like the cowboys they've circled their wagons against the Indians, to exist in an incestuous circle, living vicariously off each other. Do I join the cowboys and have a life which will be a combination of Abigail's Party and The Lost Weekend, or like Kevin Costner in Dances with Wolves, daub myself in coloured paints and go bare-back asking acceptance of the tribes?

And this is my dilemma over how I will deal with the paperback suggestion. I do like to observe life, flitting in and out of all social circles, belonging to none, but equally at home in all. I'm beginning to think that might not be possible here as the British bush telegraph stretches far and wide and yet another wrong move – such as no paperbacks thanks - could brand me a Bolshie maverick.

Actually I'm sure my card is already marked, particularly because being a journalist, I'm already deeply suspect anyway. So, I look at the letter again. Oh, bugger it, I am a Bolshie maverick – they might as well know that from the start and I pick up the phone to say as nicely as I can that I'm not coming out to play.

The woman who wrote it is Scottish and fully understands what I am saying and we finish with a vague promise to meet. Within minutes, the phone rings and another Englishman who has been helping Paul invites me to lunch with him, his wife and son. He is a tall, distracted, odd, often stammering character who has lost his job with a French company and once was an expert in reeding the roofs of Home Counties cottages. He has the burr of Kent still in his voice.

Three days later I follow his directions to another world barely 20 minutes from my open outlook. It all seems quite normal in a strange, tilted way. I am sitting on a crumbling verandah in a house dating back to the 17th century on the edge of the Gers, hidden in a lushly wooded valley, eating a very English Shepherd's pie.

Above us, stretching along the ancient columbage of the remains of another verandah, is an enormous vine, weighed down with clump after clump of black, dusty grapes. Baskets, overflowing with hazelnuts from the trees in the wild garden, are piled in a corner where the long-legged spiders cling to the wood, becalmed in the surprisingly hot autumnal sun.

Roses straggle up the walls, their colours still vibrant and their smell intense. In the valley buzzards, or possibly kites loop in a deceptively lazy vigilance ready to swoop for the kill. It is a scene straight out of Cider with Rosie, or with more people, The Darling Buds of May.

The wooden table on which sit the pie and mounds of vegetables, is a thrift-shop find; the chairs, aluminium folding garden ones; the plates and serving bowls a glorious mismatch of colour, texture and ages. It could have been styled straight from the pages of the French Country Life books I devour on their Amazon-winged arrival. Yet I know this is not artifice, this is the way they live as best as they can.

Robert is a different man here, not the diffident worker, sighing and edgy in my house as he makes a not very good job of painting my ceilings. He sprawls at the table, a beer in his hand, the man of the house - contented and at peace.

A half-smile plays on his face as he watches his young son who races around the nature-reclaimed garden throwing Frisbees to a rescued mutt, switching effortlessly from the patois of the area to a clear, beautiful and rather formal spoken English.

A few more children and the illusion of the Darling Buds would be complete. It is idyllic, pastoral, deeply satisfying with that sleepy heavy air which tries to force your eyelids shut. But all around us is evidence of the mammoth task Robert and his wife are undertaking.

Attached to the house is a drive-through barn, magnificent, but rather unsafe since storms brought the roof tumbling down; next door another half-barn now a workshop. What looks like a small cottage is quietly decaying in a corner of the grounds, but a hand-hacked flowerbed is flourishing. Brambles and rampant weeds hide a recently discovered pond and Robert paints a gorgeous picture from his mind's eye of what it will become... at some point.

After lunch we go inside to a long hall scraped back to its lime and mud origins, a suspect electrical system trailing wires, copper pipes exposed on their run up walls and ceilings. The sitting room has the echoes of a 1960s experiment with circles of brown and beige patterned wallpaper and the now expected whiff of damp.

The family live in the habitable ground floor, mainly in the large kitchen with its wood-burner, using the sitting room to watch the occasional DVD people send or lend them. Cheerfully they list the problems, the work to be done over years and years to come when and if ever, the money comes in.

They have lived this way for two and a half years, admitting to piling on the jumpers when the often icy-cold, but mercifully brief, winter arrives. They dream up ways to make money for the house while Robert awaits his official registration to work for himself and the demand based on his anticipated earnings, which will have to be paid up front.

Their fortitude humbles me. Their pride in this pile of rotten, or rotting wood still palpable despite the enormity of the work ahead and their lack of funds, makes me feel a shallow, pampered inadequate. Which of course is what I am. My greatest discomfort is a day without heating even in the autumn. My biggest horror is a tiny field mouse seen scuttling through the kitchen, or spiders bungee-jumping across my bedroom ceiling.

They talk of pine-martins fighting the cats in the hall and the edible dormice thumping around in the attic, which is not quite safe enough to access. I wouldn't last a week (night?) in their situation, but then, what I lack in guts I make up in self-knowledge and I would never have taken it on without at least £100,000 or more to fling at it.

Listening to them, I realise that despite my growing horror at their situation, their dream has already come true. They've escaped the drug and crime-ridden place they used to call home, its council blocks, its constraints and above all, its lack of hope. Here their child runs free, his life not tainted by designer trainers and roaming gangs to bully him into service no matter what his parents tell him.

At seven and a half he writes in a fluid, cursive copperplate hand, not the ugly printed letters of a British schoolboy. He willingly already spends an hour, at least, on his homework every night and more at week-ends, and finds true pleasure in flying a kite all afternoon, his dog by his side. He knows the names of all the wildlife in both French and English and dreams up imaginative ways to fill his time, a world away from a hand-held computer game. As a family they visit bastides, castles and mazes at weekends, prepare food together and discuss their days.

And at night, even if the frequent electrical storms have cut their power and left them grouped around the logburner, this little family give thanks for all they have. They sleep together in one room when the cold really bites and may often think of the superior heating and plumbing they once had. But they will never go back. What would they go back to they ask - quietly astonished at the question.

The thought of re-entering their old lives makes them both visibly shudder, and Robert's wife confirms their commitment to this wild patch with hair-raising stories of her old life in government offices in London's east end. She's been threatened, reviled, even spat on and constantly apprehensive, she lived what she now knows was a halflife. No longer, and never again she tells me with proud toss of her head.

As I leave, the child, with French formality, wishes me a grave goodbye and says he hopes to see me again. Perhaps next time, we can play a game he's made up - flicking cards into different vessels attracting different scores. 'It's very exciting,' he tells me as he gives me a demonstration of his little world and his hand-written scores on old cut cards. His age group back home would taunt and curl their lips at this simple play. I reach to smooth his handsome head, moved beyond measure. Yes, humbled is the right word for this afternoon's experience I decide, as I open my front door to the flickering message signs on the phone.

The week becomes more surreal in La France Profonde. One moment I'm discussing wattle and daub as vital to farm renovation, the next the Reagan/Thatcher love-in and by the end, fuelled by a fine Armagnac, dancing a version of Simple Simon and wiggling my ass to a French Army marching tune with three members of the Transport Corps.

It began with the pastoral lunch idyll of the Gers where I felt like an extra in The Darling Buds of May, alongside a charming couple and their son who make me feel a total capitalist pig, but also extremely thankful that I have heat and plaster-boarded walls.

Then, on returning, I am invited to dinner at the home of a couple who turned up at Las Molières a week or so ago to introduce themselves. I was out at the time and they'd upset my gatekeeper, the Blessed Brian by asking: 'Is this the home of a lonely Irishwoman?' Indignantly, as he told me when I got home, he'd sent them off by telling them: 'Miss Cook may be alone, but she is certainly not lonely.'

Bless him. Because of that presumption of sad old sod, I deliberately waited three days before I phoned the number they'd left in his reluctant hands. 'What age are they? I'd quizzed him. 'God Fidelma, I'm not good at this. About your age I suppose.'

I'd phoned them and been invited for drinks. Drinks are good. A short agreed time when you can depart relatively quickly having found potential friends, or not. I went for an hour and a half, left three hours later. Enough said.

However, the following day I did wonder if I were looking old or they were looking fabulous. 'My age? My age? He's over 70 and she's nearly bloody 70,' I told Brian, as he asked me jealously how it had gone. 'Christ, am I looking that old?' He did his down-turned meek mouth saying: 'I'm no good with ages. You look 30, honest.' What can you do?

Anyway the invitation to dinner did not make my heart sink as the others have done. He is Irish, from my own neck of the woods, with a dry, mocking wit and a mischievous abstract habit of causing mayhem with his apparently innocent questions. He was once arrested at Cheltenham racecourse, mistaken for Lord Lucan when settling into a Bentley having won a fortune from the tipsters who dubbed him M'Lord.'

Jackie is English, but with a husky laugh and a sharp, sly outrageous humour formed from years of living and working all over the world and dealing with her Frank. There's no reinvention here, just huge hearts who thirst for fun and new blood. I am new blood and surprisingly delighted to be so.

In the shadow of a large manor house, roughly four miles o'er vale and hill from Las Molières, with paper candle-lit lanterns attracting the moths on the terrace, I sit down at a crystal laden table, the smell of lamb and garlic ambrosia to my micro-waved nostrils.

Ranged around the table are a former US Ambassador, his New Yorker intellectual wife who speaks with the Streisand squeak of Brooklyn, their son, a serving US diplomat in Iraq, a former commander of troops in Northern Ireland, his Vanessa Redgrave lookalike wife and my hosts.

It is a heady combination after the simplicity of my last lunch. I think it's fair to say that in Britain it could have been a stilted, careful dinner party, crushed by the weight of expected behaviour, unless all were long and close friends. Here, it's subtly and wonderfully different. Because all have homes, mainly permanent, in France, there is chat about locals, fêtes, 'scandale,' wine, wine and more wine. It is as if, knowing there is just a big sky and a black night outside, we can all be more honest.

But then it moves on to politics – past and present. Naturally, having been outed here, all know I am a journalist and, of course, I sense a wariness, but done with such cleverness and courtesy I barely realise it until later. I choose not to 'interrogate' the American son on the situation in Iraq; I back off from asking the Maj General pertinent questions on Northern Ireland in the 70s, despite my wicked host attempting to link us to those points.

Perhaps I'm still feeling my way and don't want to test my boundaries fully in writing my column because I will find it hard to leave out what I am told. Anway, I have a great time and wend my way home in the pitch black of single-track lanes praying that the gendarmes have better things to do that night than lie in wait for a well-fed, well-wined woman trying to get used to heels again.

I have barely time to turn around before it is Sunday again and an anniversary lunch at the Blessed Brian's with his daughter, French Army son-in-law, two of his Army mates, wives and children. The second message on my answering machine.

Deliberately, after 17 years of living in France, BB and Jacqueline his wife always serve British food to the French and we sit at two tables laden with heavenly scented Guiness steak pie, potatoes and green beans. The men sit at one end - handsome, cropped-haired, truly brothers in arms. The women, voluble, good-looking, in their own world at the other. I am placed between both. The chat is fast and French, no quarter given, though BB and Jacqueline move effortlessly between both as I seek a word to translate. At one point I am reduced to saying (in

French): 'You know, I'm really much more interesting in English.'

At another, to escape my exploding 'French' head, I walk outside under the still glorious blue skies, surrounded by the pink and purple wild flowers known as Cosmos and I watch the children who had raised their cheeks to me to kiss on arrival. It is, I decide, my best ever day in France

For the first time I feel I actually am in France... privileged to be part of a family for however brief a time. A mixed family, who actually hold the key to the success of this latest English invasion. BB's daughter, Joanne, now 28, a dark-haired Deneuve younger look-alike, is no longer English. Her gestures, her attitudes, her nonchalant ease with her friends could only be French - until in answer to a question from me in English, she counters in an unmistakable Midlands accent.

At last, emboldened by the flowing wine and feeling quite sober after five delicious courses, I ask Danni sitting to my left to give me a French marching song, thinking it would be a yomping style US Marines grunt, which I have to admit I rather like. The first two he does to order are dirges, apparently common to the French Army who march off to war anticipating their death instead of their victories. Terribly dismal, as he can see by my disappointed face.

So, big body jerking, he stands at the table and moves into another gear. Which is why I came to be doing a sort of Simple Simon standing at the table (as were we all) waving arms, legs, heads and ultimately asses in the air to a repeated French chorus. I did notice it was being filmed on a state of the art mobile. Daily I am checking YouTube. So far, nothing thank God.

Chapter 15

S LOWLY, very slowly Las Molières is taking the shape I have chosen for her. The planks, timber and cheap wooden beams are being covered over and painted and along the walls the bookcases are crawling into solidity. Robert and his Moroccan side-kick who is working for £10 an hour on the black, are painting the bits with the expensive, but hopeless paint from Castorama. I know from looking at the teardrop blobs and missed sections that they are not doing it that well, but I couldn't care less at this stage, so long as they just cover it all. And once the paint is dry I can open the crates of books.

Paul spends half of the day shouting at his work: 'You're havin' a larf,' he yells at the MDF planks which defy him in their onward slide to the glass doors. 'You've got to be joking,' he screams before returning to the muttering and the plodding up and down my tiles. Cherry has finally admitted failure on the wardrobes and handed over the work to Robert, and her brief attempt at painting the first of the bookcases to be finished has been given to the

Moroccan. Instead she keeps turning up at 6pm to pick up her husband and drink my red until he downs tools at 8pm, sometimes 9pm.

It's become a bit of a ritual. Not good for her and certainly not good for me, but I do find her funny and bizarrely enjoy her company. However, Pierce is now back for a while and we have plans for actually cooking a meal. Tonight we almost got away with it, but not quite.

I need to tell this in flashbacks to make sense of it all. When Pierce got to the little white van, side down in the deep ditch at the bottom of the steep climb to Lavit, Cherry, spikey blonde hair splayed all over the steering wheel, wasn't moving; her head at an unnatural angle.

For a minute he thought she was dead, but Paul had said she and the dog were fine, but stuck. Suddenly the eyes opened, the head lifted: ''ello Pierce. Just listening to the radio.'

Behind her, the dog, scrabbling to keep her feet in the back, let out a mournful howl, strangely in tune with Paul's curses as he gazed on his loved one. As Pierce told me later, it was a curiously moving moment.

I just knew my gas-guzzling 4X4 would be vital in rural France. Without its pulling power Cherry might have been forced to listen to Radio Sud all night. No-one deserves that, even if, in speed and temper, she'd missed the bend and upended.

The evening had started relatively normally. Paul shouting: 'I don't f*****g believe it,' at the shutters he was attempting to fit to the bathroom window. The Blessed Brian plaster-boarding away, sweating heavily and Robert my new man about the house, finishing the painting of the bookcases. Pierce and I were moving into the second phase of his week's stay and he had stopped bitching and fighting long enough for me to reward him by actually cooking a meal for us both.

To this end I had peeled the potatoes. Winning the Nobel Prize for Literature would not engender the look of love and pride my son was giving me as I did such a motherly thing. What is it about men watching women do womanly things? However, I digress.

Into this scene of domestic productivity arrives Cherry in her little white van, dog panting at the back window. Paul, following a traumatic incident in a car when he was a teenager, has a phobia about driving, but can putter to work on a scooter. If tools and paint have to be moved then he is dependent on Cherry and the van dropping him off and picking him up.

Cherry's sense of time has an elastic quality that perhaps only Stephen Hawkins can understand. So instead of 3pm, she is here at 6pm, to pick up tools even though he has his scooter. A domestic ensues outside, but the upshot is that she is now sitting in the kitchen while Paul heads for a site-meeting on another job ten kilometres away, saying he'll only be 20 minutes.

Cherry needs to be here to produce the final bill, the devis for the next set of work and the percentage to be paid tonight. I don't know why. Her sums are always wrong and she admonishes her husband with the killer line: 'You know I'm no good at figures, Paul.'

Being Monday, it is my unmissable night of the week. I have two episodes of Corrie with Eastenders in between, an hour later than in Britain. And I have promised to cook a meal, which adds to the stress. This is not looking good.

So anyway, as the strains of Corrie filter into the soft French night, Cherry and I are ensconced on the sofa; Pierce is pricking holes in my supply of microwave meals for one, and there is no sign of Paul.

We have 15 minutes left of the final episode of Corrie when Paul shuffles through the door: 'Sorry about that,' he says clutching his helmet. Fifteen difficult minutes later they leave after I've told her to go home and feed her husband - my first sexist comment in 30-odd years, but France gets you that way.

She is not happy. Pierce is starving and not happy. But as I've had a few glasses of wine, I'm very happy and certainly not about to bloody cook at this late hour. So as Pierce pinpricks another micro-meal for one, his third, I light a candle on the table and sit opposite him with a large red, re-hashing the bizarre night and detailing what I had planned to try and cook.

It's me who spots the lights coming up from the crossroads. 'Probably a farmer,' I say. 'No it's not,' says Pierce, almost choking on his aromatic rice and pork, 'It's Paul's scooter.' A few seconds later we open the door. Paul, helmet off, tells us: 'I can't f*****g believe it. She's in the fosse. Can you help me mate?'

Pierce is more animated than I've seen him in months. Flinging rope over his shoulder - I have rope in my garage (?) - and he's off, with Paul scootering behind. I decide to pour another red and await their return, grateful that Pierce will not be here to go on and on about no real food.

Three quarters of an hour later Pierce is back. Pumped up on being an action hero he recounts finding Cherry, like

Marilyn Monroe, hair splayed, face down, listening to the radio while the poor dog struggles on her feet in the back. 'So, who's driving home?' I stupidly ask. 'Her. Paul can't,' says Pierce while opening the fridge to check if there is anything else to eat.

Of course. Stupid question. Twenty four hours later Cherry is back knocking on my door with Paul behind her smiling, and clutching a very fine bottle of red for Pierce. Not for me, I may add - I'm only the one who has given her glug after glug of pretty fine rouge for weeks now.

I sit her at the table and ask innocently what happened that she tanked nose first into the fosse. 'I was irritated and took the bend too fast,' she says nonchalantly, hands pushing her spiky hair upwards, grinning her silly smile.

Chapter 16

I HAVE a sick feeling in the pit of my stomach and a familiar knee-jerk desire to pull up the drawbridge or flee. Mischief is being made around me and I don't like it. So although barely ensconced in this countryside, I can already feel the suffocating, provincial tentacles stretching out to the very heart of my home.

A call has come from Cherry; a nervous, upset message on my answering machine, which I have to follow up. She and Paul should be about to leave on their first holiday in God knows how long. A holiday they deserve after years of toil. Instead, she is asking me if I have written 'bad' things about them in my column.

This is when I realise the internet has become a very personal tool - no longer the clichéd window on the world; instead a dagger which I have deliberately held towards myself and maybe now been stabbed by it.

It appears that 'someone' at the local 'international lunch club' in the area felt it her duty to tell her that I was writing a piece every week and had, the woman insinuated, insulted her husband and herself. Worse than that, her husband's professionalism. This is a club mentioned to me months ago in which I had no interest - for all the obvious reasons.

Of course the blood immediately rushes to my face; the heart pounds and I want to be anybody but me at this moment. Found out. Caught. Coward confronted. My words, my detached observations, snidey asides as they can seem if you want to read them that way, reverberating in an ether world for all to click into. A part of me wants to just press red on my phone and stop the world. Not listen to what she is asking me.

But of course I can't and mustn't. So I keep listening. In hindsight, it is interesting that this caring aside to Cherry comes after I've made critical comments on the middle-class Brit society around here. Paranoid? They do say a paranoic is only someone in full possession of all the facts.

However, that is really not the point. Cherry is hurt and she is confronting me now. I cringe and yet attack. I have deliberately made no secret to anybody I spend time with, including her and Paul, that I am writing a column about life here and so all are grist to my mill.

No-one can ever say that I was a spy in their midst; a secretive scribbler once home. Of course, there will be and are, situations, moments and all sorts of confidences that I wouldn't dream of discussing, but in the abstract I reserve the right to tell all when it touches on me.

But what is all? My take on my world and the people working for me? The people I meet who invite me to their homes? The Brits I observe with a newcomer's disdain at their loud voices and arrogant attitude?

Is all of this accurate, true, or am I simply trying to entertain in my writings? Could I stand in front of the parade of people I've met since arriving here and read out my words without blushing, stammering and failing to meet their eyes?

I have to believe I could, don't I? And so, after the first horrible moment of discovery I say to Cherry: 'You can read everything I've ever written about you and Paul. You agreed I could write about you, and I have. I believe I've done it with affection and humour.' I then tell her some of the lines I've written. She laughs and admits with good grace, 'Well, it's all true isn't it?' Truth though is no defence if a vulnerable woman like Cherry can be made to feel so upset by a 'concerned' fellow ex-pat. Or me.

'I didn't really think you'd do anything horrible,' she says, soothing me with her kindness. 'But I couldn't go away without asking you. It would have been on my mind all the time.'

Reassured by me, she says she doesn't need to read the columns. She trusts me. I put the phone down and shutter off my exposed, well-lit sitting room, longing for the anonymity of the city and its cold, uncaring stance, its indifference to all human life. And I wonder, not for the first time, what the hell I'm doing in this rural backwater where unseen eyes and ears are picking over ever look, gesture and words.

I look at my bookcases, perfectly crafted by Paul, solid and straight in this house where neither floor nor wall runs true. I remind myself that I struck lucky with Paul and all the other workers he's found for me who are bit by bit turning LM into a home, charging me a fair price and always willing to go the extra mile.

The guilt subsides, gradually. And I remember a quote, though not who said it, that in the heart of every writer there is a splinter of ice. It's true, for I'm also willing to write about my own bad behaviour – even my son's.

Perhaps there's a shaft of ice in my heart. So be it. If there are consequences then I'll just have to live with them. I decide to shutter the rest of the windows - I suddenly feel a little laid bare.

It helps that Pierce is here and I can discuss this with him. No, it doesn't really as he has no sympathy for me and asks why I feel the need to write about people I know. Obviously, I say, because that's all I bloody know. He looks at me as if I'm a little short-circuited.

I go to bed still feeling a Quisling, ashamed I've exposed Cherry to gossip and innuendo... and wondering how and when I'll break it to her that I've written about the van in the fosse episode. Thank God my friend Fiona is coming tomorrow, bringing the whiff of the city with her and her ability to put things into perspective.

Having known Pierce since he was born, she has wisely-calculated that the storm would be over and we'd both be wearily resigned to each other and capable of human communication by the time her plane landed. And it would be safe to come in.

So did I, and so optimistically invited the couple who'd had me to dine a few weeks before, for dinner the following night. Frank and Jackie. Dinner parties are the thing here to break the boredom of us non-workers.

Sustained in the knowledge of a couple of meals already behind me, I pored over the dozens of cookery books I possess simply because they're books. It took a while to find something that could be done in advance, in one pot, (in my new red cast-iron casserole pot) and then heated up. Well, several hours actually. Basically beef stew by any other name.

Driving from the airport, I told Fiona about the dinner party. A fleeting look of horror flickered across her face. She knows me so well that girl.

'You're cooking? With Pierce here? For people you don't really know?'

'Yes I am,' I said with my new French sang-froid. 'Indeed I already have. It is cooking slowly as we drive. Apparently tastes even better the next day.'

'Is that really wise?' she persisted. 'You know how stressed-out Pierce gets you and you know how stressed-out cooking gets you, so combining the two?'

'No, no,' I replied smugly. 'Not a problem as we say here.'

She stifled a pessimistic groan and moved swiftly on to Glasgow gossip. She'd already reassured me that Cherry would be perfectly happy if she were to read the columns, even the fosse one. 'It's clear you're fond of her.' With that I could think no more about it.

In hindsight it all went downhill after opening the front door. It was just after midnight and Pierce greeted us eventually, wrapped in a towel after finally having had his 'morning' bath.

'Please tell me you took the casserole out of the oven on time?' I begged with a rictus smile. 'Of course.' I pulled off the tin foil to be confronted with what looked like dried up meatballs instead of juicy d'Aquitaine 'blonde' beef chunks surrounded by onions, mushrooms and celeriac, melting in a lake of red wine, stock, lardons and herbs.

There was barely any stock left and the sprigs of thyme were like the wasted trees following a firestorm. Incapable of speech, I pulled a wizened beef bit out. It was surprisingly tender. 'It'll be fine,' soothed Fiona. 'Slosh in more wine and stock tomorrow and gently heat it.'

When tomorrow arrived, after a night in the fridge the Gordon Ramsay casserole appeared to have shrivelled even more. But whisking Fiona off for a quick tour of the area, I retained my newly-found sang-froid, telling myself all was in order and we'd be back in time for me to hydrate it, make the mustard mash and do wondrous things with the Savoy cabbage. Look, if it's good enough for Gordon Ramsay....

The guests were due at 7.30. We returned at 4.30. By 7pm I couldn't even have said 'sang-froid'; stress draped over me like a black veil, and the 'meatballs' were floating in a sea of wine and stock in an oven whose dials were incomprehensible beyond the grill sign. No heat was coming from it although it sure had the night before. Fiona tried to help, but backed off for a G and T after one look in my eyes. Pierce for once backed away too, recognising the line of sanity had been crossed, dodging out of the way as I raced to the bedroom to exchange T-shirt for silk as the wheels of a car crunched up the drive.

After meeting and greeting and seating the guests, I retired to the kitchen to prod away at the still cold stew and flick another dial before flinging canapés at them. I bashed away at the potatoes, flipped the cabbage in butter, flicked another dial, cursing every person in the other room; cursing Gordon bloody Ramsay. Cursing France and no home delivery.

At last, an hour and a half later, one switch suddenly, miraculously produced heat. From the sitting room, which in the absence of food had become a red-wine black hole, came the sound of cheering as I yelled: 'Not long now.' Gulping a quick rouge myself, my blood ran cold as I heard another, horribly familiar sound. Pierce in full flood; in argumentative mood where every polite conversational gambit is greeted with a: 'Really? Actually I think that's absolute rubbish... if you'll forgive me saying so.' At that point I knew he was not going to play nicely tonight. In the circumstances I poured another, large, glass of red for me before handing another bottle into the black-hole.

Pierce was now discussing the lack of French resistance in World War Two, their basic cowardice allied to their semi-Fascist leanings and also, by the way, their inability to produce good beef because they were incapable of hanging it properly. Frank and Jackie, my new very best friends, were yelling at him as if he were a grandson. Fiona was silent, coming out every so often to see if I were still in the kitchen and hadn't just wandered away into the fields.

When they finally sat down they were all so grateful for any food they even had second helpings. Even Pierce shut up long enough to eat and was obviously enjoying my stewed meat in all its complex favours. Gradually I relaxed, feeling the storm clouds drift away from my head as my sang-froid slowly returned watching my new friends eat up. I beamed at my guests who were making a real good fist of eating dinner at 10.30pm and even dared nod at them in complicit understanding of a rather special night.

And then, through the buzz of conversation at the far end of the table as I slide into candle-lit happy-cooking bliss I hear a loud question: 'Did you know my mother does a column in a newspaper? She'll write about tonight, you know. She writes about everything that happens to her.'

Happy that all eyes are on him now, including my bulging glazed shut the hell up ones, he spears a chunk of the blond d'Aquitaine my columns have bought and says matter of factly: 'Oh yes, I've warned her I'll sue her if she writes about me again. It's not on, you know. You should all be aware of what she does. She twists things. I'm not saying they're not true, they are but they're... well, twisted.

'She's very good at that, but she doesn't care who she writes about and who reads it. She's a typical journalist, no qualms about invading anybody's privacy, even her own. So I'm warning you for the future. If I were you, I'd tell her you'll sue if she mentions you.' He chews on as all slowly stop eating.

I catch his eye, as all eyes catch me. I am Medusa. But sadly, he does not turn to stone. Instead he says, astonished at the silence he has created and my death stare: 'What? What? It's true, isn't it?'

Yes my dear, it is. So bloody sue.

Two days later when I drive both Fiona and Pierce to the airport we can laugh about that night. 'Well at least you know you've still got it,' she says. 'You won't go completely native so long as you can still write.'

I think about that to block out the melancholy I always feel when left at airports as others fly back to what is still to me 'real' life. For I'm slightly worried that I've already gone a little bit native and rural France could be a very dangerous place for a woman alone.

Not dangerous in the sense of thieves and predators. No, something far more insidious than that - a rhythm, a disturbing undercurrent of life which gently seduces and then corrupts all previous boundaries.

There are days here when I achieve nothing at all, don't even attempt to and feel no guilt whatsoever. It has become vitally important to me to re-read all the French classics, to rediscover Sartre and de Beauvoir and dip back into Molly Keane, for Irish relief.

Some days I don't go further than the tin mail box at the end of the drive. On others I speak to nobody, my only human communication via the internet and e-mail. I've taken to talking a lot to Portia like some mad old biddy – even answering for her sometimes.

Most mornings begin with coffee and a 'read' through the papers on screen. If I waken early, I'm repaid by watching the dawn rise in a magnificent blood-red sun, or scan the mists that turn the valley into a mysterious monochromatic painting.

For now, I'm interrupted only by the Blessed Brian, who is slowly and painfully working his way through the plasterboarding. He lifts huge panels of the stuff into the sitting room, clearing a space at the end of the day so I can switch on the TV and drown out the long night. Paul and Cherry have gone on to other jobs, other houses, no doubt entertaining nervous newcomers as they once did me.

On days when Brian doesn't come, the house - and me - are suspended in a crisp, silent, visually beautiful ochre world of surrounding fields harrowed and planted awaiting next spring. I understand the phrase 'all's right with the world' as the land seems to orderly proceed towards the closing of the year, closing itself down in preparation for its inevitable regeneration.

Invitations to parties in Glasgow and London arrive and I look at them as if peering through a telescope the wrong way. It's friends' way of keeping me in the loop, particularly the newspaper jollies. Of course I could leave here for a while, barring the shutters, kennelling Portia, clicking the easyJet flight. Once there, sipping the office champagne and hearing all the gossip I could even pretend to myself I was still in the loop, still valued and part of it all, even though I know no-one gives those who've gone a second thought.

But it all seems too much trouble, too overwhelmingly tiring to contemplate, so I wedge another log into the wood-burner, pour another red and lie back on the sofa in happy anticipation of returning to my book.

When friends ring with tales of who did what to whom, who did what at what party, I no longer nit-pick the details. Instead, unlike last year when I was miserably installed in the English countryside, I wonder how they can bear to keep doing the same old things, going to the same annual parties with the same 100 faces. I feel myself drifting above such things as if they're happening in another world, far, far away. Which of course they are.

The dark introspection, which hit me on occasions as I languished in ugly provincial hotels on the search for this house has mellowed into a strange self-knowledge that neither disturbs nor worries me. Such serenity though still doesn't extend to the night and the light stays on in my bathroom.

Portia too lies around in blissful disarray, rarely rising before noon, tuned in to the farmers' vans passing on their way to lunch. A sprint after each and every one in her new country dog mode, a check on the policies and back she comes for her afternoon nap. Often she stretches in her sleep, luxuriating in her once unimaginable freedom.

Now, with no more guests expected, even my newly-acquired basic cookery skills can go into hibernation as the microwave works instead, or the frying pan hisses with the frozen sauté potatoes and fried eggs that are becoming a mainstay as the weather cools.

I am so detached that I missed Portia's weekly grooming day because until mid-day I was certain it was Sunday. In fact every day seems like Sunday now when there is no work, bar the column, to tick off my hours; no boss to phone to update my progress on this or that story; no contacts to meet and squeeze for stories they don't realise they're carrying.

Which is why rural France is a very dangerous place. Hidden, just out of sight, is a little pile of estimates and bank statements. I do not need to open them to know what they say. There's the credit card bill on which I've had to put the BB's final payments; the local bank statement showing the disappearing figures, chunks taken out to pay in cash the painting and the work on the garden which has been taken out of Jean Pierre's reluctant hands and given to a young man who comes to mow not to philosophise.

There's the estimate for the guttering and drainage which if I accept will require 30 per cent up front of money, which is no longer there. The estimate for running sisal up my miller's stair and into the study and Pierce's bedroom – which I simply have to have to cover the remaining ugly, badly stained planks.

In the stable the massive oil tank filled barely a month ago is already half-empty as I keep my powerful radiators blasting out an average temperature of 20 degrees, sauna temperatures to the Brits around here who know to the penny what they can spend if they're to keep within the bounds of their fixed income.

And tomorrow, having incredibly deciphered my 'books' and final accounts, my accountant will give me a rough idea of what I have to pay. In a rare moment of forward planning I set aside a sum for this day. I have nibbled into it a bit, of course, and even my own limited arithmetic tells me there will not be enough to pay what will be demanded.

For an hour or two I can feel quite dispirited and a touch fearful as to where I will get all this money. I need to be working, seeking out stories, even story ideas, need to shake off this happy indolence, stop gazing into the mists or lying on sofas reading between snoozing.

But not yet dear God, not yet. After all, it may be that I don't owe as much tax as I think and what's left over can pay for the work and the sisal. And by not going back for parties, I'm only spending on my own fags and booze.

It's tiring doing financial planning so I put another log on the fire, open my latest Amazon delivery and ponder what to read first. Indeed, this is a very dangerous place for a woman alone and far too happy about it.

Chapter 17

THE scent of sweet pine permeates my dining room. The white vans of the farmers stop at the crossroads, and the swarthy drivers peer from a distance at my Christmas tree, which fills the French windows at the heart of Las Molières, lights ablaze in a once-forgotten farmhouse.

My shutters are thrown open and candles flicker in the windows. Mario's 'Joy to the World' rings out at high volume on the CD player as I dance from room to room, ticking my boxes of perfect Christmas joy.

The Blessed Brian and his box of tools packed up last week. There is nothing more to be done. Well, no more money left for anything major to be done. Las Molières is as finished as she can be.

The guest room is now a white painted and plaster-boarded haven; the ugly stall divider long gone, the manger covered with bookcasing. One wall has two simple, but effective white Ikea wardrobes, which Cherry never got her hands on thank God. Lamps soften the whiteness compounded by the linen on the French rattan bed, as do the paintings and a bundle of magazines lying on the coffee table between two checked armchairs.

The wood in the hall is covered too and the large round, glass-topped, full-skirted table is filled with photographs from my life - Pierce's face changing from round-faced blonde boy to angular handsome man. Mine, changing from round faced blonde woman to round faced blonde old woman.

The sisal running up the stairs and throughout the top floor unifies the once messy arrangement and in the sitting room the chimney breast, where the bare bulb dangled out from, is now filled with the gilt-framed mirror.

Books and paintings fill the walls and on the gun table silver trays hold decanters and bottles. More photographs fill the two other small tables and books on French design and gardens lie by rank on the kelim stool. Logs are stacked either side of the wood-burner, its flames ruby red through the window.

Silk shaded lamps picked for a far grander drawing room adapt themselves surprisingly well to this much humbler dwelling, shining on Christmas cards sent by the little group of friends I have already made here. Also adapting itself well is one of the pair of chandeliers, which fits perfectly in its high spot among the beams.

But it is the kitchen/dining room that shows the most startling improvement, a combination of art gallery with my collection of black and white art on the wall above the manger, and library from the bookcasing perfectly hugging two walls. At the dividing half-wall of the kitchen, my little silver collection gleams on a Georgian side-table facing the elm table which looks as if it were made for here. Above it the large eight-candled wrought iron chandalier.

I have piled pine-cones, clementines and life-like fake ivy and fir branches on the divider, with heavy pillar candles ready to be lit. And in front of the glass doors, the tree dripping with the decorations of years past, presents beautifully wrapped by the French assistants under its heavy boughs, pinprick bulbs of white light shining down.

I cannot wait for others to see it as I do now. Laura, a young friend and talented writer for the Mail on Sunday and her husband Steve who plan to fly from London, then drive from Barcelona on Christmas Eve, armed with my only request - oat cakes and biscuits for cheese. (Well, hopefully also with a crate of wine from Spain, even cheaper than here.) Pierce arrives tomorrow, in time to quiz me on the arrangements and please God, approve them all.

Christmas Eve should be gloriously simple here. I have ordered a platter - a feast - of seafood. Oysters, lobster, crab, langoustines, queenies and all sorts of other bits from the amazing fish counter at Leclerc, the supermarket a mere 20 miles away.

They bring in men and women to cook and prepare the fruits de mer on the day for collection at the last minute. It is the French tradition to celebrate Christmas Eve with seafood, though few wait until after Midnight Mass to eat as was the custom many years ago. You simply discuss with the fishmonger the number of guests, the presentation and decide on a price. For us four I have agreed a total 'luxury' budget of roughly £50. I dread to think what it would cost in Scotland.

They will add in a number of sauces, all hand-made by

the same men and women toiling in the back. I will simply add in salads, bread and maybe an exquisite tarte, also hand-made, from the local patisserie. The wine, even the Champagne, will be a quarter of what it would be back home. As, disgracefully, will the whisky.

I hope we will end the night sober enough to drive the 4 km to Lavit and midnight Mass... well, hopefully one of us will be sober enough to drive. I want to stand outside the mediaeval church shaking hands and wishing everybody a Joyeux Noël in the crisp night air before returning, to LM where the fire burns on and the tree lights beckon us in.

On Christmas Day I will serve up foie gras and sweet white wine, followed by a guinea fowl capon safe in the knowledge that Steve, an excellent cook, will keep me right in what I'm doing. I have champagne sorbet and amuse-bouches in the freezer, a chocolate log in the fridge and wedges of cheese, all locally made in artisan farmhouses.

For the first time in years I am totally organised and calm. It had become a joke that I was always flying back from somewhere on Christmas Eve desperate to get back in time to shop. One year coming from Bosnia I landed in Scotland on the last plane in, having neither food nor presents in the house and Pierce just one plane ahead of me. But in a city even on Christmas Day there is always an open shop.

I have also planned an 'open house' on Boxing Day, having invited all my French farming neighbours for a house warming. I did this by carefully putting the 'time from' on Christmas cards, which I hand-delivered up every track. Most French send New Year greetings that can arrive any time until the end of January. All seemed somewhat bemused by my card and long-winded explanation of open house, which is a mystery to them.

Apparently so is a buffet, which I had originally thought of doing. Countrymen and women do not understand the concept of a meal taken standing up. They need a plate, knife and fork and a seat at the table from which they will not move until all the food has been taken in its correct order. Piling hot, cold, fish, meat on one plate as we do is considered both bizarre and barbaric.

They do understand aperitifs. So I'll need to have loads of 'bits' (again, simple to order in advance) so that they will stand and chat with the odd Brit who still talks to me and all the men who have worked on the house, their wives and us.

A couple of old hands here tell me they'll probably not turn up. Apparently other 'Anglos' have tried it and no one came or even apologised for not coming. I think, hope, my neighbours might. If only to see inside what was once a tiny farmhouse with, it now seems, a long history. The French may pretend to be above curiosity, but they're still only human.

Last week, I met a man who knew some of the story of my house. He told me that ten years ago it was bought by a French couple a week after it went on the market. It had been put up for sale immediately after the funeral of an 85-year-old woman who had been born here and would not allow it to be sold in her lifetime even though it was quietly crumbling away. She could not bear to part with it.

It seems Las Molières was the humble dwelling, which spawned a modest farming estate and the woman and her descendants went on to bigger, more comfortable houses leaving the old house to fend for itself.

As a child she would have lived with her parents and

siblings in the two rooms which are now my sitting room and bedroom. Warmth would have come from the adjacent stables and byres with humans and cows literally and openly side-by-side in my now dining room and kitchen. My study and Pierce's bedroom was the hayloft. The rest did not exist, and the lavatory was an outhouse with a long drop.

I'm told she loved this place with a passion and her eyes were always turned towards it and her heart never left, but even so, she would rather see it fade away than let it go from the family.

Although most likely post-Revolution, the house's big oak beams were apparently re-claimed from grander houses destroyed in the peasants' revolt - carried home in triumph as a share of the spoils.

In the main 'mother' beam in my sitting room ceiling there is a deep heart shaped hole. I thought it was a delightful quirk of nature. Now I am not so sure. Perhaps my old lady's ancestor whittled the filched oak to mark his place here before erecting his 'new' house.

For their sake, particularly hers, I promise to love LM more. Tonight in the mellow hush before my favourite time, I feel I will.

On Christmas Eve as the four of us sit, champagne in hand before the fire, I re-tell the story, dramatically pointing to the heart as the finale. We all smile at each other, anticipating the feast to come, which is sitting on top of my car in the cold night air, cellophane wrapped on a bed of ice - waiting to be opened straight to table.

The table is laid, the foie gras softening on the side and even Pierce has a contented look as he sprawls in his chair.

Laura, champagne glass in hand, teeters off in her kitten heels to run a bath and wash her hair, reluctantly leaving the fire and the sofa.

Her piercing scream cut through our reverie. She was standing at the bathroom door, a look of pure horror on her face. Steve pushed past her and reeled back out saying: 'Christ.' Pierce and I were next. The bath was half-filled with ominous brown sludge, which was gurgling up from the plug-hole. Merde. Indeed. Even for urbanites like us, it didn't take long for the centime to drop. Then we all shrieked and ran back out, slamming the door as we went.

Somehow, somewhere the fosse septique was blocked. It was the only answer. Yet Gloria had told me I had the Rolls Royce of fosse septiques newly-installed, which had left me smugly confident when hearing similar tales.

Remembering I'd seen a plunger somewhere in the garage, we decided to try plunging. Well Pierce and Steve did. Laura and I went back to the champagne and agreed it mightn't be wise to use the other bath - just in case. After several messy attempts the men gave up and re-shut the door. Reluctantly I phoned the Blessed Brian, apologising for interrupting his Christmas Eve and seeking his advice. He told us to use as little water as possible and he'd be here in the morning to sort us out.

Feeling immeasurably cheered by his words we agreed to ignore that bathroom and settled to our crustacean mountain. Only Steve seemed to be immune to thoughts of what might be going on down the corridor, concentrating on trying every shelled creature. Pierce decided the huge platter was off-putting, and Laura and I played around with the lobster, shuddering every so often.

On Christmas Day morning, the Blessed Brian lives up to his name and arrives to look at the situation. We go with him and peer into the bath which had drained overnight, leaving a greasy, unmistakeable gunge in its wake.

After tinkering with an array of plungers and head-shaking a lot at the plumbing, he breaks the news that there is nothing he can do and warns us not to run water down the sinks or use the loos. Use a basin for the washing up and throw it out. No baths, no showers, catch the water in a flannel and make do with a rub-down.

As we were already aware we were in crisis, we'd started early, very early, on the Bucks Fizz. The guinea fowl is in the oven and a ton of vegetables is ready for preparing. And oh yes, I'm giving a party for 35 people the following day. Joy to the bloody world.

Looking at my ashen face under the alcohol flush, Brian eventually concedes we can use one loo as little as possible, but warns he isn't sure how long it will take before the bath 'refills.' Well they say you can always take the measure of a man, or woman, as to how they behave when things are going badly.

Laura, Steve and I find that old Dunkirk spirit and prepare to manage. Pierce is ready to check out, find an hotel with a good restaurant and send me the bill. The Dunkirk spirit saves the day. Aided by copious amounts of exceptionally good wine and the perfection of the roasted bird, we wassail as we wash even the roasting dishes in a tiny bowl, ferrying back and forth to fling the contents on the grass. The men use the fields, which they love doing anyway and Laura and I practice self-restraint, and the bath doesn't refill till late evening.

On Boxing Day morning it has disappeared again and we still couldn't raise a plumber. Party or cancel? Looking at the mountain of bought-in canapés, the filled fridge and the crates of wine, my creative decorations, there is only one option. Party. But go buy plastic glasses and paper plates I tell Laura and Steve while I scrub the bath. And go to the loo while you're out.

Thank God I did. The farmers and their wives all come bearing flowers and wine, dressed in their Sunday best, pleasantly shocked at the changes to Las Molières, warmly welcoming me to the fold. I wait until the last of the guests arrive then call them to attention.

It is not the welcoming speech I had intended to make in my best French. I had visualised myself, hair gleaming, in full party dress, graciously raising a glass of champagne to the workers who had done so much to make the place almost perfect in time for Christmas; to my farming neighbours who had all responded to my invitation and to the fellow émigrés who had received me with advice and hospitality.

Instead, hair unwashed for three days, un-showered and slightly mad-eyed, I am telling the men to pee in the field and the women to hold off as long as possible and definitely not wash their hands afterwards. I apologise for the plastic glasses, telling them they have to drink from something which can be thrown out afterwards as there is only so much can be done with a washing-up bowl. Nobody seems at all surprised, just sorry that it's happened to me.

Several hours later and after a guest whispers in my ear, I have to make another speech telling them the main and only working bathroom is now blocked. The sight of floating sewage in a pristine white bath is a little off-putting I find after a few canapés.

I look around the room at this mix of people, only three of whom I knew more than six months ago and let the sound of French and English wash over me.

Paul is in a corner launching into one of his stories, Cherry on best behaviour urging him on. The BB, looking like a white elf in his chinos and jumper is quietly getting sozzled. Kate, a serene woman who came here with her partner who sadly died barely two years into his long planned venture. Genevieve who farms for her parents across the hill and represents the Tarn et Garonne on high level farming problems in Montauban and Paris.

Ann, the book swop woman from Aberdeen and her husband Dave, now bringing back to life an old house in Montgaillard. Absent are Frank and Jackie, in England with their family.

And my neighbours, all rather alike with good-humoured faces, who all seem to be related. My nearest neighbour is Letitia, a fey, shy and very attractive 30-odd year old who lives with her young sons in a rented house. I see Pierce circling her, closing in gradually, his face dropping as he realises she doesn't understand a word he's wooing her with. It is a good group of people.

I become aware that Pierrot, another neighbour has been investigating by flashlight my piping leading to the tank, along with Pascal, a friend of Paul's, when they return shaking their heads and pull me to one side.

It seems the pipework to the tank has been installed by what can only have been a deranged, drunk, or spatially-challenged fitter. Or a willing amateur who'd lost his

Braille DIY instructions. There were no inspection hatches to open in tracing the block and to compound the problem it looks as if the filters of the tank itself are completely sanded up with the contents ready to explode on to my garden.

What will I do, I asked? Nothing says Pierrot, patting my arm. 'I'll be here tomorrow and I'll sort it for you.' He seems taken aback by my gushing thanks and disappears off with a formal handshake.

Gradually there are only us four left to hold a post-mortem on the success of the day and the wisdom of going through with it. In the bathroom, the sludge line shows no sign of diminishing.

As promised Pierrot returns. Refusing all help he digs trenches in the courtyard until he finds the blockage. We hear the sludge surge out. After lunch he returns with Marc, a neighbour I somehow missed in the invitations and a sluicing machine to evacuate the tank. We useless townies sit inside and do what we do best - mix Buck's Fizz.

They come inside at my insistence when finished, pulling off their now filthy overalls and washing their hands. They accept a drink, but refuse all payment, even the bottle of whisky and cognac I offer as a thank you. We're neighbours, he explains as if to a simpleton and neighbours help each other. Laughing he says they have a saying that neighbours are cousins and I'm his cousin.

Glasgow feels very far away as we four re-hash this later and realise how little we know of good neighbourliness or even how little we remember. I wonder if I'll ever be able to do something for him and Miriam, his partner, in return.

'Stick 'em in your column,' says Pierce grinning. And I do.

And now I'm alone again. All have returned for New Year parties that hold no thrall for me anymore and I contemplate the year behind me and what is to come, though that is more of a sideways squint. I never like to think too far ahead, superstitiously never planning anything in advance, crossing fingers, touching wood, invoking God to be willing, that I will still be here. Not here at Las Molières, just here - still breathing.

Perhaps that's strange for an optimist who believes in the glass half-full. It is not simply because I am middle-aged with very bad habits which may indicate an early demise. No, I have done this all my life – never, ever tempting the fates.

I prefer to spend Hogmanay alone, calmly seeing the year switch over with a television countdown. Probably because on the few occasions in the past when I have gone out, I've tended to get rather over-excited and disgraced myself, barely registering the moving of the clock hand.

Looking back anyway is always positive - well, for an optimist it is. The bad gets air-brushed and explained away. In the past 12 months my life has changed in ways which, still astonish and catch me by surprise. Like when I walk out of this house and see the Pyrenees etched on the southern skyline and a buzzard perched on a fence post, registering my presence with arrogant, cold indifference.

There are moments when, for no reason, I am suddenly chilled by the knowledge that in many ways I am in an alien world as indifferent as that buzzard to my presence.

There are moments too when I wonder how I've ended

up here and think fondly of my old life and my friends just a gossip away. But now I cannot recall when I last fervently, desperately wanted that life back, or walked in memory through my West End flat.

The past year is already blurring and without the columns to remind me, I would have forgotten or possibly erased the abject misery I felt in the search for Las Molières. I cannot now summon up the bleak, black loneliness and fear of that first night in the Lavit flat waiting for the keys of a house, which suddenly seemed both ugly and repellent. That burning conviction that I had made the biggest mistake of my life.

I can only recall it dimly and acknowledge it happened because I wrote about it. I can no longer feel it and isn't that a good thing?

More and more I'm learning to live in the moment. To give in to my natural indolence and do absolutely nothing all day. To acknowledge I can actually feel joy in silly, simple things like recognising a woodpecker sitting on the lawn, or feel my heart lift as I drive into the valley when the clouds are so low, the hills stand as tall as the Alps.

Oh, bugger all that, even if true. I would still kill for a Ho Wong yuk sung, a Mother India's garlic chilli chicken and a massive steaming portion of fish, chips and mushy peas.

I would love to grab a black cab and head to a good Italian restaurant to meet my Glasgow pals in real streets with lighting and people shouting, fighting, laughing.

On the way I would flash a glance at open lit windows, not the shuttered, silent houses I pass on my way 'home.' I'd even enjoy the banter from the driver, tipping him without converting back into sterling. Sure of my coins and my place. Sigh. However, in the end nothing really changes, only the setting. As I prepare to draw the veil on this year, I've had my quick squint into the next.

Oh dear, oh dear... it is not looking good - on first squint anyway. The little bit of cash has totally gone, spent on making Las Molières comfortably acceptable. The tax bill is in - way, way over what I put aside. I've organised a (rare) overdraft at the local bank and I have maxed out on one credit card. Forget the important drains and guttering. Everyone has damp here.

Were I a pessimist, I would be downhearted. Probably rather terrified at having no cloth to cut. Cross with myself for never learning my lesson and blithely carrying on as if I had a salary and prospects.

But I'm not. I'm an optimist and I know, just know, something will turn up. Even if it doesn't, what larks Pip!

Ah well, there should be interesting times ahead at Las Molières - God willing.

Acknowledgements

I OWE an enormous debt of thanks to all my friends, both old and new, who got me here and keep me here. The ones who truly wish only the best for me whatever I may do. Real and much-loved friends.

I must also thank The Herald for commissioning the column, which forms the basis of this book, its readers who urge me on in e-mail missives, and Norman Macdonald who believed in it.

And of course, my noblest friend of all - Portia.